access to philosophy

RELIGION *and* SCIENCE

Mel Thompson

Hodder Murray

A MEMBER OF THE HODDER HEADLINE GROUP

Some other titles in the series:

Ethical Theory 2nd Edition
Mel Thompson   ISBN 978 0 340 88344 0

Philosophy of Religion 2nd Edition
Peter Cole   ISBN 978 0 340 81503 8

Sex and Relationships
Michael Wilcockson   ISBN 978 0 340 72489 7

Environmental Ethics
Joe Walker   ISBN 978 0 340 75770 3

Orders: please contact Bookpoint Ltd, 130 Milton Park, Abingdon, Oxon OX14 4SB. Telephone: (44) 01235 827720, Fax: (44) 01235 400454. Lines are open from 9.00–5.00, Monday to Saturday, with a 24 hour message answer service. You can also order through our website: www.hoddereducation.co.uk

British Library Cataloguing in Publication Data
A catalogue for this title is available from the British Library

ISBN-10: 0 340 75771 X
ISBN-13: 978 0 340 75771 0

First published 2000
Impression number   10 9 8 7
Year   2006

Cover photo from Science Photo Library

Typeset by Transet Limited, Coventry, England.
Printed in Great Britain for Hodder Murray, an imprint of Hodder Education, a member of the Hodder Headline Group, 338 Euston Road, London NW1 3BH by CPI Bath.

Contents

Preface

To the General Reader

Although *Access* books have been designed mainly to meet the needs of examination students, they also have much to offer the general reader. *Access* authors are committed to writing up-to-date scholarly texts in an easily accessible format. The main body of the text should therefore provide a readable and engaging survey of the subject, in easily digestible sections. Clarity is further enhanced by sub-headings and bulletpoints.

To the Student Reader

Access books are written mainly for students studying for examinations at higher level, particularly GCE Advanced Subsidiary (AS) Level and Advanced (A) Level as well as the Scottish National Qualifications in RMPS at Intermediate 2 and Higher Levels. A number of features have been included to assist students, such as the word-lists at the beginning of chapters and the material at the end of chapters.

To use this book most effectively, you should be aware of the following features.

- The introductory chapter will set the scene for the material in the rest of the book.
- If you turn to the relevant chapters, you will find that they are broken down into sub-headings and bulletpoints. There are sometimes also Key Issues to focus your attention on important points.
- The Key Words at the beginning of each chapter are for easy reference and to help you become more familiar with the technical language of the subject.
- At the end of each chapter is a Summary of the main points, presented either as lists or diagrams. This is a useful quick revision tool. The list can also form the outline of your own notes on the topic.
- There may be some suggestions for further reading on the topic.
- There is also a range of typical examination questions, with some specific advice on how to answer them. Do tackle the specimen questions, planning your answers to some of them and writing some in full.

General advice on answering essay questions

Structured questions will tell you what to include. The following advice is for those questions which leave it to you to work out.

- The most important thing is to read the question carefully and work out what it really means. Make sure you understand all the words in the question (you may need to check some of them in the dictionary or look up technical terms in the Word Lists in the book).
- Gather the relevant information for answering the question. You will probably *not* need everything you know on the topic. Keep to what the question is asking.
- Organise your material by drawing up a plan of paragraphs. Make sure that each paragraph is relevant to the question. Include different views within your answer (most questions require arguments for and against).
- Start with an introduction which explains in your own words what the question is asking and defines any technical words. Work through your answer in your carefully planned paragraphs. Write a brief conclusion in which you sum up your answer to the question (without repeating everything in the essay).

NOTE This book replaces *ATP 7: Religion and Science* in Hodder & Stoughton's *Advanced Teaching Pack* series. It contains much of the text from the Student's Booklet from that pack, updated where appropriate. It also contains some, but not all, of the information given in the Teacher's Notes, and on the Worksheets. Those who have copies of that pack may find its survey of publications still of value (although now rather dated, of course), along with its background notes for teachers. The Worksheets may also be used alongside this book where appropriate.

Introduction

> The eventual goal of Science is to provide a single theory that describes the whole universe.
>
> *A Brief History of Time*, Stephen Hawking, 1998

Modern science offers a wonderful vision of the world, from the idea of the universe expanding outwards from an original 'big bang', to the nuclear forces within an atom. The complexity of things we take for granted, like the amount of genetic information needed to construct a human body, is quite astounding. The sheer dimensions of the universe revealed by modern cosmology, as we look out into space on events the light from which started its journey towards us even before our planet was formed, stretch our imagination.

Science also challenges our assumptions. It is a discipline that deliberately examines and questions evidence. What may seem obvious to one generation is questioned by the next. Above all, science works its way towards a total understanding of the world – an ultimate goal, which (in practical terms) it will probably never be able to fulfil.

On the other hand, there is so much represented by the broad term 'religion' that science cannot address: intuitions about the meaning and purpose of life, a sense of being 'at home' in the universe, and convictions about what is morally right.

A majority of people still claim to belong, at least nominally, to a religion. Even where interest in organised religion has diminished, the intuitions about life and its meaning, the sense of wonder and of celebration, which in previous generations would have been expressed largely through the medium of religion, are still very much in evidence. To see how these relate to the scientific world view is as crucial an issue now as ever.

1 The interface of religion and science

It is possible to define the areas of interest of religion and science in such a way that they do not conflict with one another. In 1925, A N Whitehead suggested:

> Science is concerned with the general conditions which are observed to regulate physical phenomena; whereas religion is wholly wrapped up in the contemplation of moral and aesthetic values. On the one side there is the law of gravitation, and on the other the contemplation of the beauty of holiness. What one side sees, the other misses; and vice versa.
>
> *Science and the Modern World*

But this view (which has a long history) does not do justice to the fact that both religion and science offer views of the world and overall ways of understanding it. Science, in setting out the general conditions of physical phenomena, thereby makes claims about the nature of the world and of life which are relevant to human beings and their religious impulses. Equally, religion is seldom prepared to limit what it says to the areas of morality and aesthetics.

Religion is a very broad term; we need to be more specific. Some religions have no problem with science. For example, Buddhism is based on the investigation of phenomena, and is not dogmatic. It has a view of the world that corresponds very closely with the modern scientific view, and where it appears to make claims that science might challenge, it offers them only as guidelines, not as dogmas to be accepted without question.

On the other hand, the Western theistic religions – Judaism, Christianity and Islam – are all dogmatic, in that they have doctrines to which believers are required to subscribe. A person cannot, for example, be regarded as a Christian without beliefs (whether expressed conservatively or radically) in the existence of God, the divinity and resurrection of Christ, and the hope of Eternal Life or personal resurrection. Equally, it would be difficult to be Christian and not accept the idea of miracles or the effectiveness of prayer. Radical theologians may try to re–interpret doctrines to make them compatible with modern world views, but such interpretations are by no means universally accepted. To be a believer requires a commitment to accept certain things as true, and to see the world as created by God. A similar case could be made for both Judaism and Islam, for both are grounded in a theistic view of the world, a view which has enormous implications for understanding oneself and the world.

What is more, all the major religions speak of a fundamental reality, which they see as underlying everything we experience:

- *Torah* (Law) – in Judaism
- *Logos* (Word) – in Christianity
- *Shariah* (Law) – in Islam
- *Dharma* (Reality or Teaching) – in Hinduism
- *Shunyata* (Emptiness) – in Mahayana Buddhism

In other words, they claim to be dealing with and to be based on something fundamental to the way the world is. This inevitably brings them, and their claims, into the scientific arena.

2 Clinging to old ways of seeing

In examining the debates between religion and science, it is important to maintain a historical perspective. Christianity originated at a time when people's view of the world was very different from that revealed by modern science. Ideas about God, the supernatural, miracles or demonic forces as the cause of illness, unremarkable two thousand years ago, may cause problems for people today. Those who shaped the early doctrines of the Church were influenced by the best available philosophy of their day, Augustine of Hippo was deeply impressed by neo–Platonic thought and the 13th century theologian Aquinas used the newly rediscovered ideas of Aristotle. Their ideas were therefore closely linked with the general views of their time.

The problem with this is that ideas and philosophies of a previous age become embedded in scriptures and creeds and arguments, and therefore appear to be endorsed by religious authority. Thus new interpretations of the universe (e.g. from Galileo) appeared to conflict with earlier philosophical views which had become intertwined with Christian doctrine, and therefore appeared as an attack on religion itself.

With the Renaissance and Reformation, the authority of religious doctrines was challenged. Secular philosophy and secular science emerged, although often through the work of those who would have described themselves as religious. By the 18th century, philosophers like Hume could question the evidence for miracles in a radical way. His arguments were not science, but they were made possible because of an environment in which it was natural to question such things.

Religion has responded in a number of ways to the challenge of science. Some Christians have argued that the Bible must be right and therefore science (if it disagrees) must be wrong. Hence there are those who try to show that the world was created as described in Genesis. Others have tried to reinterpret Christianity in ways which show its beliefs to be compatible with science.

Such reinterpretations are not new, nor are they necessarily disloyal to the Christian tradition. A first century Christian would have struggled to understand the views of Aquinas (13th century), and would have been totally incredulous when faced with the kind of mechanical world accepted by Christians in the 18th century as proof of God's creative design. The outrageous heresy of one generation may well become the accepted belief for the next. Few Christians today would want to argue that the Sun revolves around the Earth, or that, by divine influence, blood seeps from one side of the heart to the other, but at one time they might have felt obliged to do so!

3 Relevance

One problem is that science has not always explained or explored its relevance. Professor Erwin Schrödinger (most widely known for his illustration of one of the dilemmas of Quantum Theory in a puzzle known as 'Schrödinger's Cat') offered a sound piece of advice to scientists in a lecture given in 1950:

> Never lose sight of the role your particular subject has within the great performance of the tragi–comedy of human life; keep in touch with life – not so much with practical life as with the ideal background of life, which is ever so much more important; and, *keep life in touch with you.* If you cannot – in the long run – tell everyone what you have been doing, your doing has been worthless.
>
> E Schrödinger *Science and Humanism*, CUP, 1950

But equally, religion has sometimes focused too narrowly on doctrinal formulae, and set aside the breadth of its spiritual quest. A N Whitehead, put it thus:

> Religion is the vision of something which stands beyond, behind, and within, the passing flux of immediate things; something which is real, and yet waiting to be realised; something which is a remote possibility, and yet the greatest of present facts; something that gives meaning to all that passes, and yet eludes apprehension; something whose possession is the final goal, and yet is beyond all reach; something which is the ultimate ideal, and the hopeless quest.
>
> *Science and the Modern World*, p238

Whitehead thus saw religion as an overall, integrating, personal view of life, giving meaning and purpose to the ever–changing multiplicity of things.

4 Change and commitment

Nobody would dream of saying that science was threatened or destroyed by the new ideas put forward by Einstein or Darwin. Rather, these thinkers represent a step forward for science. Well established theories are tested out and modified; eventually they may need to be scrapped and replaced; this is the way science makes progress. With religion, however, beliefs are held for very deeply personal reasons, or because they express the identity of a particular group of people; challenges to those beliefs are therefore often resisted. This is a fundamental difference between science and religion.

The nature of commitment is also different. In religion, commitment is often made to a particular belief, or even more narrowly to a particular way of expressing a belief, a form of words or a creed. In science, the commitment is generally given to the scientific quest itself, rather than to any one particular theory.

Of course, there are cases of scientists becoming committed to particular theories, but, in the long run, science is based on evidence, and a scientist who holds a view that goes against that evidence is likely to be challenged for acting in an 'unscientific' way. Here again, we come up against a fundamental difference between religion and science.

5 Balancing religion and science

Religion and science have much to offer one another. In the words of Albert Einstein:

> Science without religion is lame
> Religion without science is blind.

Those engaged in science may benefit from exploring the general questions about meaning and purpose that are raised by religion. This is particularly true in terms of the ethical and environmental consequences of scientific advances, for example. Without some sense of direction or purpose, science loses its impetus. It has been argued that one should seek knowledge for knowledge's sake. In practice this has almost never been the case. Knowledge has quickly been utilised for other purposes, whether for weapons of war, or new medical techniques.

Equally, it would be most unwise for religious believers to try to keep their beliefs separated from the general understanding of the world that informs everyday life. For its own health, it needs to be informed and even challenged, by science.

1 From the Greeks to the Medieval World

KEYWORDS

atomism – the theory that all substances are composed of atoms and space

efficient cause – that which is the agent of change

final cause – the purpose, or product of a process of change

Form – Platonic term for a universal, of which particulars are merely copies

deduction – the process of drawing conclusions from general principles rather than by observation and experiment

metaphysics – the study of the general principles and nature of reality

essence – that which makes a thing what it is; its fundamental nature

For 1,500 years, the Christian view of the world had been so influenced by the Greek philosophers Plato and Aristotle that their ideas and those of Christianity had seemed inseparable. Their thought provided an intellectual structure within which Christian doctrines were expressed and through which they were defended.

As background to the issues of science and religion, we therefore need to start by looking at the earliest scientific explorations of the Greeks, at Plato and Aristotle, and finally at the Medieval world view which dominated Western religious thinking prior to the rise of modern science.

1 Pre-Socratic theories

The earliest Greek philosophers (generally known as the 'Pre-Socratics' since they taught before the very influential period of Socrates, Plato and Aristotle), were concerned to develop general theories to explain the nature of things.

The earliest of these, **Thales (6th century BCE)** came to the remarkable view that all matter – substances of very different sorts, solid or liquid – was ultimately reducible to a single element, and mistakenly (although understandably, considering how widespread it is) thought this element was water. What was remarkable was not his conclusion but his quest; the idea that everything can be analysed to find a common element. Equally astounding was the insight of **Heraclitus (also 6th century BCE)** that everything is in a state of flux, things may appear to be permanent, but in fact everything is subject to change.

Leucippus and Democritus (5th century BCE) developed a theory known as **atomism**, which suggested that all matter was comprised of very small particles separated by empty space. This, remarkable in its anticipation of modern science, implied that individual things, and the materials of which they were made, took on their character by the form, or organisation, of the atoms of which they were comprised. In other words, here was a theory of matter that saw different sorts of substance as representing various combinations of a single basic feature, the atom.

They saw that substances can change – water becoming ice or steam – and recognised this as evidence for a common, atomic basis for all three. It is difficult to overemphasise what a remarkable achievement this was. Moving from observation to the formulation of an underlying theory, these pre-Socratic philosophers were doing what we would clearly recognise as science.

2 Plato

KEY ISSUES
- The doctrine of the Forms
- The priority of eternal universals over concrete particulars

---

Plato argued that the things we see and experience around us are only copies of unseen eternal realities. Thus the tree that I see in front of me is a particular example of an ideal, perfect tree. I know it to be a tree because I have an intuition of that ideal tree – indeed, it is the eternal and ideal tree that leads us to the notion 'tree' in the first place. Therefore, in order to understand the world, a person has to look **beyond** the particular and examine the most general and universal.

In his famous analogy of the cave, most people do not see things as they really are, but merely as a set of fleeting images, shadows cast on a wall as objects are passed in front of a fire. The philosopher sees beyond the fire, through the mouth of the cave, to the light of the sun. Reality is only understood by turning away from the wall and its shadows (the phenomena we experience) and making a difficult journey out of the cave and into the world of eternal and unchanging Forms.

The key feature here is that there are two very different worlds, the world of the Forms, ideal and perfect, and the imperfect, transient world of our everyday experience. The religious person, like the philosopher, is encouraged to turn away from the latter in order to appreciate the former.

Notice what far reaching implications this has for religion and science. For Plato, the concept or idea is more real than the particular things experienced. When Christianity was influenced by Platonic thought, it therefore claimed that its doctrines represented a reality, compared with which knowledge of this world was but a pale shadow. This is the very opposite of the scientific approach, which is empirical – i.e. it is based on experience.

3 Aristotle

KEY ISSUES
- The classification of the sciences
- Efficient and final causality
- The authority of Aristotle for Aquinas

Aristotle (384–322 BCE) took a very different approach from that of Plato. He argued that our knowledge of the world comes through experience interpreted by reason. In other words, you need to examine phenomena, not turn away from them.

In line with this view, it was Aristotle who classified the different sciences. He also introduced the term 'metaphysics' for those sections in his work that came after those on physics – and these dealt with the more general issues of the structure of thought, as opposed to the examination of experience.

The process of scientific thinking therefore owes more to Aristotle than to Plato, although, as we shall see later, the authority given to Aristotle's ideas was a hindrance to the development of science. The basic assumption about how knowledge is gained, and the relationship between things perceived and the more general ideas to which they give rise (i.e. the distinction between science and metaphysics) stems from Aristotle.

a) The Four Causes

Aristotle considered that things had four different types of causes. These are best appreciated by considering the example of someone chipping away at a block of stone in order to produce a sculpture:

1. The stone itself is the **material cause** of the sculpture.
2. The emerging shape of the chipped stone is the **formal cause** of the sculpture.
3. The person chipping away is the **efficient cause** of the sculpture.
4. The sculpture itself is the **final cause** of what is taking place. It represents the purpose and intention behind the activity of the sculptor in doing the work.

Of these, the **efficient cause** is the one most often considered; indeed, in ordinary language, to cause something is to be the agent of bringing it about.

For Christian ideas about God, however, the idea of a **final cause** became important, for it suggested that everything had its place and purpose in God's final plan.

> **Example:**
> If someone has fallen seriously ill, a person who believes in God may ask 'Why has this happened?' Clearly, he or she is not expecting an answer in terms of **efficient causality** (in other words, about viral infection or other medical conditions), but **final causality**: not what conditions have brought it about, but what its purpose is. In other words, the person is expecting that the illness will have some final cause, perhaps in order to teach someone something, or to give them an opportunity to display certain qualities. The more tragic and pointless the suffering, the more difficult it becomes to see that it has a 'final cause'. Unlike the sculpture, there is no apparently beautiful end product, only a heap of stone caused by apparently destructive and random chipping. This is the basis of the religious 'problem of evil.'

It is important to recognise that for Aristotle, **all four** causes were included in the description of an object. When we come to look at the rise of modern science in the 17th century we shall see that the universe was thought of as a huge, impersonal mechanism, operating according to fixed laws. These laws considered material objects, their relations to one another and the forces operating upon them. It tended to overlook the idea of purpose in its analysis, relegating it to a more general idea of the purpose given by an external creator, God.

b) Unmoved movers

Aristotle argued that everything was caused by something else, which in turn was caused by yet something else again. But can you have an infinite sequence of causes? In theory it is possible, but in practice, you can never know that a sequence is infinite, the most you can say is that it **appears** to have no end. Thus there are no actual infinities, only theoretical ones.

Therefore Aristotle's philosophy leaves open the possibility of an unmoved mover (or uncaused cause), responsible for all movement in the universe, and the cause of all that exists. However, it would be equally possible for the world to be infinite and eternal – needing no uncaused cause, because it would have no starting point and no boundary.

The 13th century philosopher and theologian, Thomas Aquinas, was to use Aristotle's argument about the possibility of an unmoved mover to present his cosmological argument for the existence of God. He was using arguments and concepts set down by Aristotle, but whereas Aristotle could conceive of an infinite world, Aquinas could not. For if the world is infinite and eternal, there is no need to posit a creator – indeed the idea of creation makes no sense if the world is eternal. Aquinas could not accept that possibility, and therefore opted for the idea of the uncaused cause.

> **NOTE** for Aristotle and the other philosophers of this period, there was no distinction between philosophy and science. Reason applied to experience was both science and philosophy. Indeed, it was only with its increasing specialisation that science became separated from philosophy. Until the 19th century, physics was generally called 'natural philosophy', a term still found today in some traditional university departments.

4 Shaping the medieval world view

> **KEY ISSUE**
> - The combination of Greek thought, Ptolemaic cosmology and Christian doctrine, provide an overall view of the world, endorsed by religious authority

a) Ptolemy of Alexandria (2nd Century CE)

Medieval Christian culture had a view of the world which was based partly on biblical imagery and partly on a mixture of Plato, Aristotle and the cosmology of Ptolemy of Alexandria.

In this cosmology, the Earth was at the centre of the universe, surrounded by glassy spheres on which were located the moving planets and the fixed stars. There were 10 spheres in all, seven for the known heavenly bodies, an eighth for the stars, an invisible ninth which moved the others, and a tenth which was the abode of God.

All movement was controlled by spiritual forces, and this led to an interest in astrology, since each sphere was thought to influence events on the Earth. Everything in the spheres above the Moon was perfect and unchanging. God's power was believed to filter down to Earth through the influence of these heavenly bodies.

The Earth itself was thought to be made up of four elements – earth, water, air and fire – each of which had a natural level, with earth sinking down and fire rising up. So motion was explained in terms of the natural tendency of the elements.

There was also a distinction between motion on Earth and that in the heavens. The heavens were perfect, and motion therefore had to follow a perfect form – namely, it had to be circular. This belief was later to prove an obstacle to scientists, not merely in the view that planetary motion had to be circular, but also by opposing the idea put forward by Harvey that blood was pumped around the body by the heart. Such circular movement of blood could not be accepted as true, for circular motion was only appropriate in the heavenly realms, not on Earth!

Notice that such arguments were deductive. In other words, they started with a theory and then examined what facts ought to follow from it. Contrast this with an inductive argument, as used by science, where evidence is gathered and a theory framed in order to explain it.

b) St. Augustine of Hippo (354–430)

St Augustine was a hugely influential Christian writer, but for our purposes we need to notice just two things that particularly influence later issues in religion and science.

- He was convinced that, since God was the creator, something of his nature should be seen within his creation – even though that creation was 'fallen'. In particular he saw God reflected in what he considered to be the highest feature of the created order: human reason.
- The second, which was taken up by Aquinas and others, was that the wonder people feel in examining the natural world should lead on naturally to a worship of God, its creator.

These, as we shall see, are basic to what is known as the 'argument from design'. Taken together they imply a view of the world as rational and purposeful, and which moves from rationality, beauty and purpose to an acknowledgement of the existence and creativity of God. But the divine order is quite separate from the ever changing material realm. Like Plato, he makes a clear distinction between the eternal and the temporal.

c) The Kalam Argument

Until the 13th century, the works of Aristotle were not widely known in the Christian West. His re-introduction into mainstream Christian thinking only took place with the work of Aquinas (see below). But before that time, an argument for the existence of God was developed by the Muslim philosophers al-Kindi (9th century) and al-Ghazali (11th century), which reflects the philosophy of Aristotle, which had been preserved in Arabic translation.

The argument may be set out as follows:

- everything that begins to exist must have a cause for its existence
- the universe began to exist
- therefore the universe must have had a cause.

This argument is based on the idea that, although you can have a theoretical infinite, you cannot have an actual infinite. It is impossible to show an infinite succession of causes, stretching back into the past. At some point, it was argued, there must have been a situation where the universe either could have or could not have come into existence. But al-Ghazali argued that in situations where one of two things can happen, neither being absolutely determined, what actually happens will depend upon the will and choice of a personal agent. This agent must be God.

The Kalam approach is interesting from the perspective of the philosophy of religion, but it also has implications for a consideration of the relationship between religion and science. For Islam, Allah is the supreme creative source of everything, omnipotent and omnipresent. What the Kalam argument says is that we cannot continue a series of causal explanations for ever. Therefore, although individual things within the universe can be explained in terms of causes that precede them, the universe itself cannot be so explained, but must come through the personal choice of God.

Not everyone would agree. One might argue that, where two possibilities are equally likely, things happen at random, without any personal choice, or that an actual infinite is possible, although we can never prove it. Or one might argue that causality is circular (perpetual motion), with the universe being like the inner surface of a sphere, so that you can travel for ever, crossing and re-crossing your tracks, but never coming to an end.

However, notice that what you have here is the insertion of a religious concept (God) into a logical argument about the structure of the universe. In other words, **God is used to explain the universe's structure**, and – once this is done – there is the danger that, for a person who wishes to continue to believe in God, there will be a temptation to accept only those explanations of the universe that give scope for God to have such a place.

This became an important feature of much of the later debate between religion and science. **Once you structure God into your science, then belief in him will predispose you to accept one scientific explanation rather than another.**

d) Thomas Aquinas (1224–1274)

The influence of Aquinas on subsequent Christian teaching, especially within the Roman Catholic Church, has been immense. He is best known for his '5 ways', put forward as arguments for the existence of God. In these he attempted to use concepts developed by Aristotle, especially his idea of final causes and of the uncaused cause, to show that a logical examination of agreed facts about the world led to the conclusion that God existed as an unmoved mover, an uncaused cause.

In this, Aquinas was fortunate in going to work in universities at exactly the time when Aristotle's works were starting to be rediscovered again in the West, mostly translated from Arabic. Aquinas thus used what was considered to be the best natural philosophy of his day as a foundation for his Christian beliefs.

In terms of this medieval synthesis of natural philosophy and Christian doctrine, it is probably the equivalent of a theologian today taking arguments about what happened at the 'big bang' to explain God in terms of the developing structure of the universe. Whatever is meant by 'God', in Aquinas' terms, is integral to his whole understanding of the structure of reality. In his thought there is no sudden move from natural philosophy to religion – the one leads on into the other.

Thus, for Aquinas, the exploration of the final cause of something – the natural purpose and function it has within the whole scheme of things – only serves to confirm his view of divine providence. He used the analogy of an arrow speeding to its target. The arrow, being inanimate, cannot have intelligence or purpose. Therefore the purposive nature of its flight indicates the action of an intelligent archer. If inanimate things thus seem to work together for some purpose, there must be a creator and designer: God. Value and purpose – established through the use of Aristotelian logic concerning final causality – is now given religious authority.

When the medieval person looked up to the stars, set in fixed crystalline spheres, he or she saw meaning and significance because the Earth was at the centre of the universe, and the life of mankind was the special object of God's concern.

Since Aristotle's 'unmoved mover', there has been the assumption that the universe has a cause and an explanation beyond itself. It lies behind the Cosmological arguments of Aquinas, the eighteenth century arguments about design, and the desire of some religious thinkers to find a direction and rational purpose to evolutionary change.

A rational universe, established by an 'unmoved mover', protects the human mind against the despair and nihilism of a world where everything is a product of chance. It offers a sense of ultimate meaning and purpose to human life.

But the key question, as we encounter the newly emerging science, is simply this: does such a world view square with the facts?

5 Religion and the rise of science

KEY ISSUE
- The Christian religion provided a view of the natural order that encouraged the rise of science, but an authoritative attitude that hindered it

For Plato, the unseen 'Forms' were more real than the individual things that could be known through the senses. This way of thinking (backed by religion) led to the idea that reason and the concepts of perfection could determine what existed, and that any observations which appeared to contradict this must automatically be wrong.

As we shall see in the next chapter, astronomy gives examples of this. Copernicus (1473–1543) and later Galileo (1564–1642) were to offer a view of the universe in which the Earth revolved around the Sun, rather than vice versa. Their view was opposed by those whose idea of the universe came from Ptolemy and in which the Earth was surrounded by glassy spheres – perfect shapes, conveying the Sun, Moon and planets in perfect circular motion. Their work was challenged (and Galileo condemned) not because their observations were found to be at fault, but because they had trusted their observations, rather than deciding beforehand what should be the case. Kepler (1571–1630) concluded that the orbit of Mars was elliptical, whereas all heavenly motion was thought to be perfect, and therefore circular.

These astronomers were struggling against a background of religious authority which gave Greek notions of perfection priority over observations and experimental evidence. In other words, the earlier medieval system of thought was 'deductive' – it deduced what should happen from its ideas, in contrast to the later 'inductive' method of arriving at a theory from observation.

However, there were exceptions to this. The most notable of these was **Roger Bacon (1220–1292)**, who based his work on observation, and criticised the tendency to accept authority or custom as a sole reason to believe something to be true, a view that caused great controversy in his day. Among many other things, he set down ideas for developing flying machines, and his work on optics led to the invention of spectacles.

There are features of the medieval world view that are important for understanding the rise of science and its relationship to religion. The Christian religion, as expressed in the medieval synthesis, promoted the views that:

- The world is created good and is therefore worth examining. (In other words, it was not a totally other-worldly religion, despising the physical.)
- God had made the world in a rational and ordered way, and thus it is capable of being understood correctly by human reason.
- Nature should not be worshipped in itself. It is not holy and untouchable. Therefore it may be examined and, if necessary, changed.
- Humankind had been given the right to 'subdue the earth' in the book of Genesis, and this would justify the development of technologies for human advancement.

When we come to look at some of the figures prominent in the rise of science, we will find that many of them are religious. Indeed, when the Royal Society was formed, seventy percent of its members were Puritans, for whom religion was of supreme importance. For them, Christian teachings provided impetus for and justification of their scientific work.

The only thing to notice, however, was that Christian theology in the medieval period had become wedded to the philosophy of Aristotle. In other words, those who were to defend Christian teaching against the rise of new science were actually defending an old natural philosophy against a new one, for an attack on Aristotle appeared to imply an attack on Christian teaching itself.

Notice also that medieval thought, following the influence of Aristotle (whose work was taught in universities throughout Europe from about 1250), was based on looking at essences and potentials.

You asked what the essence of something was, and you then asked about its final purpose, how it could make its potential into something actual. The world was not (as in later centuries) seen as a collection of matter pushed and pulled by various forces, but as a collection of things created with a particular essence and seeking their final purpose and fulfilment. Fire had an innate tendency to rise up and water to flow down, acorns found their final purpose in the oak tree into which they might grow. **It was a philosophy that fitted well with religion, since purpose and essence were central to both.**

Although it is tempting to contrast the medieval world with that of the rise of science in the 17th and 18th centuries, it would be a mistake to underestimate the way in which medieval thinkers and institutions made later science possible. The 13th century in particular saw a great flowering of philosophy and science, and the establishment of universities throughout Europe, with 'natural philosophy' taught within the faculty of arts. This was an important preparation for later developments in both philosophy and science.

Summary List

- Early Greek thinkers seek an overall theory to account for the world
- Plato points away from particulars to universals
- Aristotle bases his studies on observation and categorises the sciences
- Augustine sees reason and beauty as pointing beyond the world to its creator
- The medieval world view combines Ptolemy's cosmology with Aristotle's philosophy and Christian doctrine
- The medieval tendency to deductive thinking and the authority of Aristotle and the Church, become an obstacle to new thinking based on observation and experiment.

Essay Questions

1. Compare and contrast the philosophies of Plato and Aristotle in terms of their influence on the medieval world view and the religion of the period.

   (The key issue here is the Platonic tendency to look for the ideal and the universal beyond the world of experience, contrasted with the Aristotelian tendency to seek final causes within it. Each with its own particular religious implications.)

2. Does the medieval world view require the existence of God in order to make sense?

3. To what extent might it be argued that science is based on a fascination with the world, and religion on a fascination with what lies beyond it?

   (One could answer this with particular reference to the views of the world prior to the rise of modern science. It would be useful to contrast Plato and Aristotle, showing that natural philosophy could take either a this-worldly or other-worldly view.)

2 The Rise of Science

1 Astronomy

> **KEY ISSUE**
> * The conflict between theories based on observation and those backed by the authority of the Church

Copernicus (1473–1543) was a Polish priest who did not consider that his science conflicted in any way with his religion. His main work was on the movement of the heavenly bodies: *De Revolutionibus Orbium*. In it he claimed:

1 that the Sun was at the centre of the universe
2 that the Earth rotated every day and revolved around the Sun once a year.

This seemed to dethrone the Earth from its position in the centre of the universe, making it difficult to see why humanity should have cosmic significance. Copernicus also noted that there was no stella parallax (i.e. no shift in the relative position of the stars when viewed from two different places on Earth) and therefore correctly estimated that the stars must be considerably further away from the Earth than was the Sun. Clearly, such findings conflicted with the cosmology of Ptolemy, which had become an integral part of the Christian view of the universe.

When his book was published, a preface by the Lutheran theologian Osiander suggested that Copernicus was merely offering a more convenient and useful way of thinking about the universe, without claiming that his cosmology represented the way things **actually** were. (In other words: 'We know, through divine revelation, that the world is actually like X, but it might be useful, to help with our calculations, to think of it as like Y.') This rather sad preface is clearly recognising that religious authority might feel threatened by the development of new theories based on observation and reason rather than on an unquestioning acceptance of the authority of ancient thinkers. Instead of confronting that as an issue, it side-steps.

However, two principles were established by Copernicus' work, which are important for understanding religion and science issues:

1 he established that scientific theories should be formulated on the basis of carefully gathered evidence
2 his work implied that ideas established by the ancient Greeks, and which had become incorporated into Christian religious thinking, might actually be wrong.

This last point is most important. Christian thinking had identified itself with a particular philosophy, such that any challenge to that philosophy was regarded as a challenge to itself. Defending Christianity and defending Aristotle became linked in a way that brought Christianity into unnecessary conflict with the emerging sciences.

Although Copernicus appeared to challenge tradition with his heliocentric view of the world, he remained very Aristotelian in his thought. Asked why, if the Earth revolved, things would not fly off, he replied that evil effects could not follow from a natural movement. Asked why there was no constant wind because of the Earth's motion, he replied that the atmosphere, because it contained 'earthiness' (one of the four elements) revolved in sympathy with the Earth itself. These are Aristotelian answers. Later (as we shall see) Newton would have explained such things through gravity and the laws of motion, but Copernicus has not made the move into that sort of thinking.

Brahe (1546–1601) observed a new star in 1572. This may not seem remarkable today, but remember that, from the medieval perspective, all above the Moon was perfect and unchanging. He had observed what the prevailing theory said could not happen.

Kepler (1571–1630) used both observation and mathematics to formulate the laws of planetary motion. He found a time difference between what he observed and what he calculated should be the case. The conclusion he came to was that the orbit of the planet Mars was not circular at all, but elliptical, with the Sun at one focus of that ellipse.

This was a radical break with Aristotelian thought. Aristotle accepted the idea that perfect motion was circular; therefore the heavenly bodies must move in circles. Earlier astronomers, including Copernicus, had made their observations of non-circular orbits conform to Aristotle, by saying that the orbits were in fact **epicycles**. (An epicycle is the path of a point on one circle as it rolls around a larger circle.)

Bruno (1548–1600) moved a stage further in challenging religious authority with speculative ideas based on the new cosmology. He read Copernicus in the 1580s and came to the conclusion that, since the Earth went round the Sun, the distinction between earthly and heavenly no longer applied. He declared that the universe could be infinite, and that there might be innumerable inhabited planets like ours. He then moved on to religious speculations based on such a cosmology, claiming that there could be many other incarnations and redemptions for those living on other planets. Such views clearly ran counter to Christian teaching, and the Church responded forcefully; Giordano Bruno was tortured to death in 1600.

2 Galileo

KEY ISSUES
- The issue of authority
- The Book of Scripture and the Book of Nature

The developments in astronomy that had been taking place since the time of Copernicus came to a head, as far as the religion and science debate is concerned, with the work of **Galileo (1564–1642)**, whom Einstein regarded as 'the father of modern physics'. He demonstrated that the forces of nature work in a regular, mathematical way. He also observed four moons orbiting Jupiter, thus making a total of eleven heavenly bodies rather than the traditional seven. He believed that the Earth moved round the Sun, and was a heavenly body like any other. His book *The Message from the Stars* was published in 1610.

In 1616, the Holy Office declared that it was 'revealed truth' (i.e. found in the Scriptures) that the Sun moved round the Earth, and Galileo's view was therefore condemned.

In 1632, Galileo went on to publish his *Dialogue of the Two Chief World Systems* in which he compared Copernicus' view with the traditional one based on Aristotle and Ptolemy. He came to the conclusion that Copernicus was right, and moreover claimed that Copernicus had described the actual universe and not simply offered a useful alternative way of making calculations (which is the guise under which Copernicus himself had put forward his ideas).

Galileo was put on trial and forced to recant. He was condemned because he challenged the literal interpretation of scripture, and the authority of the Catholic Church. In its place he had set reason and observation. To do so appeared to eliminate from science any place for providence or spiritual influence.

Galileo's trial marks a very negative turning point in the relationship between religion and science, and a breakdown of the medieval synthesis.

He had established two important scientific principles:

* that change comes about through efficient rather than final causality (to use Aristotle's terminology); objects do not seek a goal that lies in the future, but are moved by previously existing forces
* that the universe can be explained in terms of mathematical principles.

This did not mean that Galileo was not religious. His own view (which was put forward also by Francis Bacon) was that God had provided two different but complementary ways of looking at the world and understanding God: one through scripture and the other through nature. Those who condemned him would not allow the second of these to contradict a literal interpretation of the first.

COMMENT There is a certain irony in looking back at this debate between Galileo and the Inquisition. Galileo said that the sun was fixed and that the earth moved. The Inquisition said that the earth was fixed and the sun moved. That was the principal difference between them. From the standpoint of relativity, however, Galileo was (strictly speaking) no more correct than the Inquisition. The sun and the earth move relative to one another. Which moves round the other is simply a matter of perspective. The crucial difference was that Galileo was prepared to consider a perspective that did not place humankind at the centre of things.

---

3 Francis Bacon

KEY ISSUE
* The criteria for science

Francis Bacon (1561–1626) rejected Aristotle's idea of final causes, and insisted that knowledge should be based on a process of induction, which is the systematic method of coming to general conclusions on the basis of evidence about individual instances that have been observed. He warned about 'idols': those things that tend to lead a person astray. They included:

- the desire to accept that which confirms what we already believe
- distortions resulting from our habitual ways of thinking
- muddles that come through our use of language (e.g. using the same word for different things, and then assuming that they must be one and the same)
- believing things out of allegiance to a particular school of thought.

Bacon also warned that, in gathering evidence, one should not just seek those examples that confirm a particular theory, but should actively seek out and accept the force of contrary examples. After centuries of using evidence to confirm what was already known by dogma or reason, this was quite revolutionary.

> **NOTE**   Francis Bacon should not be confused with Roger Bacon, who taught in Oxford during the flowering of science and culture in the 13th century, although they shared similar views on the place of reason and experiment – views which were at the forefront of progressive thinking in the early 17th century, but were quite astounding for someone writing 350 years earlier.

4 Newton

> **KEY ISSUES**
> - The establishment of Newtonian physics
> - The place of God in the Newtonian scheme

Sir Isaac Newton (1642–1727) devised a system of physical laws which explained planetary motion, refining concepts such as mass, force, velocity and acceleration. He claimed that everything would continue in motion in a straight line unless acted upon by forces. Therefore the world moved and changed according to fixed laws and, once started, would continue to do so without further external influence. Thus – to put it crudely – he presented the image of the world as a mechanism, which, once set in motion, would continue to move in ways that were predictable and reflected its construction.

This overall approach – which was hugely influential and successful, dominating science for almost two hundred years – had two enormous implications for religion:

1 Aristotle thought that divine spirits impelled things to seek their natural purpose or end. This was the cause of movement, without which everything would remain at rest. Newton had provided an alternative explanation for movement. What is more, he saw motion on Earth and in the heavens as fundamentally the same (whereas in the medieval scheme of things they were quite different, the latter being perfect and circular).

2 Although the idea of God might be useful for explaining how the world started, it was not needed to explain its continuing existence and motion, since all was a natural working out of previous causes, following mathematical principles. Mathematics could predict motion.

Newton's most influential book was *The Mathematical Principles of Natural Philosophy* (1687).

Newton himself was religious, and he used an argument from design – namely that God lay behind, designed and guaranteed the mechanistic world. The world may work on mathematical principles, but God had provided those principles. Newton was also not above occasionally making reference to God in order to explain unusual phenomena – thus he invoked divine influence to explain variations from the predicted in planetary motion. (Later, Laplace was to re-calculate their orbits and, when challenged to show how God was influencing them, famously said 'I have no need of that hypothesis.') On the other hand, he was fully in line with the principles set earlier by Galileo and Bacon, that the 'Two Books' of nature and scripture should be seen as separate but complementary.

a) Christianity less mysterious

During the 17th century there was a fundamental shift in attitude away from the idea that God might be revealed in the irregularities of nature – the miracles and the mysterious – to a sense that a creation that was not regular, mechanically sound and working with mathematical precision, was not worthy of a divine creator. This led to an emphasis on rational religion, devoid of superstition (as set out, for example, in Toland's *Christianity Not Mysterious*, 1696), to deism (the belief in an external creator god who is not personally or actively involved in his creation) and to the popularity of Newton's argument from design.

b) Science more threatening

Prior to the 17th century, 'pagan studies' (as science was seen by the Church) was largely a matter of rediscovering ancient texts, and was limited to the very few people who received a university education, but from then on books and ideas were more widely spread through the population. Also, following the Reformation, Protestants enjoyed a greater freedom to study the Scriptures, and to trust individual reason rather than imposed authority in their interpretation.

These factors gave discussion of religion and science a social and political edge. The illogical defence of traditional positions, so difficult to appreciate from a modern perspective, might well have been motivated by a desire for stability and order in a world that seemed to be sinking into free-thinking anarchy. However, Protestants were as ready to condemn new scientific findings as Catholics. Both Luther and Melanchthon personally condemned Copernicus, and the Protestant astronomer Kepler took refuge with the Jesuits to escape persecution.

However, it should be emphasised that the majority of those engaged in science thought of themselves, like Copernicus and Newton, as theologically orthodox, and hoped to show that their scientific findings were compatible with Christian doctrine.

5 Primary and secondary qualities

> **KEY ISSUE**
> ● How you relate primary qualities (number, size, shape, duration) to the secondary qualities (colour, sound, smell, touch) by which human beings experience their world

The philosopher **John Locke (1632–1704)** took an empiricist view of the theory of knowledge; in other words, he believed that everything we know comes from sense experience. But he recognised that there was a difference between perceiving shape, for example, and colour. He therefore divided the qualities ascribed to an object into two categories: primary and secondary. The distinction was clear:

● **primary qualities** belonged to the object itself, and did not vary according to the way in which it was perceived, something had a particular mass and was in a particular location
● **secondary qualities** depended upon the faculties of the person perceiving them, or the circumstances in which they were perceived.

Thus, for example, colour, smell and sound depend upon our faculties. As the light changes, or if it grows dark, the colours we see will also change; the phenomenon of colour says something about our perception, not about a quality that can be fixed and ascribed to an object. Science therefore attempted to reduce everything to primary qualities that could be measured, and which seemed to be objective and fixed.

Let us look for a moment at the implication this has for the scientific view of the world. Light is analysed into waves or particles; sound into vibrations, or changes in air pressure. Our experience of the sound, as something beautiful, or being at a particular pitch, was no longer seen as the 'real' description. Sound was **really** just a set of vibrations; only becoming what we experience as sound, through the working of our ears. The mechanical world of Newtonian physics was therefore a strange and rather dull place. The 20th century philosopher A N Whitehead, commenting on the implications of 17th century science, said:

Thus nature gets credit for what should in truth be reserved for ourselves: the rose for its scent: the nightingale for its song; and the sun for its radiance. The poets are entirely mistaken. They should address their lyrics to themselves, and should turn them into odes of self-congratulation on the excellency of the human mind. Nature is a dull affair, soundless, scentless, colourless; merely the hurrying of material, endlessly, meaninglessly.

However you disguise it, this is the practical outcome of the characteristic scientific philosophy which closed the seventeenth century.

Science and the Modern World, A N Whitehead

This has enormous implications for such issues as freedom and determinism, miracles, design, or anything which concerns a religious or personal interpretation of experience. The perception of the world that took shape during the 17th century, and which was exemplified in the physics of Newton, was fundamentally materialist and mechanistic. It was a world formed out of the concepts (mass, location and energy) that scientists have abstracted from their overall experience.

These abstractions – the dull, grey hurrying of matter, as Whitehead was to call it – were the result of highly abstract reasoning. But they were successful, in that these abstract concepts could be used to predict behaviour, and thus could be used in science and technology.

They had mathematical precision, simply because they were based on mathematics (see section 7, below). The crucial thing to recognise, from the standpoint of the history of the interaction between science and religion, is that **they were mistaken for reality**. The abstract notion of sound waves became seen as more 'real' than the music they described. The universe became, in the popular mind, **identified with** this impersonal, mathematically predictable mechanism that scientists had abstracted from their experience.

Example:

I may play a CD whose music moves me to tears, and yet – from the perspective of a narrowly defined science based on primary qualities – I am told that what is 'real' is not the music at all, but the sequence of digital information on the disk. But that is not the whole story for, as Richard Dawkins points out in *Unweaving the Rainbow*, there is a sense of wonder that comes with appreciating the complexity of what is analysed. It is not that the digits are real and the music is not, rather that the wonder of science is in seeing the way in which the digits can and do transmit and reproduce what we experience as beautiful music.

The problem is that, if you have a world in which everything from atoms to stars is blindly following its patterned course, obeying impersonal laws, the more complex organisms (including human beings) start to be regarded in the same way. I can have no freedom or purpose in anything I do, simply because, in the mechanistic universe, every action is already fixed and determined.

In the 19th century, this view influenced ethical thinkers like J S Mill, who saw human volition as determined by their motives, and those motives could be expressed in terms of the conditions that brought them about. In other words, the **experience** of freedom had no place in the analysis of what caused that action. We shall return to this issue in more detail in chapter 8. For now, it is important to recognise that its origin lies in the way in which the scientists and philosophers of the 17th and 18th centuries identified abstract ideas with reality itself.

6 The new thinking

During the 18th century, as part of the whole movement that was outlined above, we find the development of philosophies that reflected the new spirit. Both in Britain and on the Continent there were developments in philosophy and a new appreciation of the place of reason in life. This new movement is generally referred to as the **Enlightenment**.

One example of this new spirit is found in **David Hume (1711–1776)**, the Scottish philosopher particularly known for his empiricism (the view that all knowledge starts with sense experience) and whose argument about miracles appears on page 93. He presented a challenge to even the most cherished of religious concepts at that time – the idea of God as the designer of the universe.

a) The design argument

Many Christians of this period argued that the predictable and ordered world shown by Newton, illustrated that the world was the handiwork of an intelligent designer. In 1802, William Paley published his *Natural Theology*, in which he argued that, if one were to find a watch upon the ground, one would assume – by the intricate way in which its parts were fitted together to produce movement, and that, were anything to be positioned differently, it would fail to work – that it had an intelligent designer. So too, he argued, the world displayed a sense of design which necessitated an intelligent designer – God.

Hume, by founding all knowledge on experience, had earlier criticised this popular notion of design. He argued that, in a situation where there are a vast number of possibilities, only those that actually work will survive. Therefore what appears now as the product of an external intelligent designer may in fact be the one surviving example of a large number of variations – surviving because it was the one that worked and stabilised. Hence you could have the appearance of design without an external designer.

b) Deism

The new, rational view of the universe allowed for an external designer god, evidenced by both the fact of the world's existence and the intricacies of its design. Such a god, however, was not expected to interact with the world, in the sense of being personally involved, or setting aside the 'laws of nature' in order to produce miracles. Belief in such an external designer god is generally termed 'deism'.

In contrast to deism, some religious groups concentrated on the personal and emotional aspects of religion, and were unconcerned by the new mechanistic views of the universe. These included the Methodists in England and the Pietists in Germany. For them religion and science were separate spheres of life and they had no need to argue from one to the other.

c) The implication of Hume's criticism

The design argument enabled 18th century rationalists to accept a place for religion. The implication of Hume's criticism was that design did not require a religious explanation, and therefore (like Laplace and his calculation of the planetary orbits) he no longer needed to use God to explain what was observed.

This simple but devastating argument sets the tone for later debates, most notably over Darwin's theory of natural selection. Hume's argument (that given a very large number of possibilities, that which works will survive) is effectively given a specific mechanism in natural selection. In its 20th century version, given random genetic damage, only those new genes that are successfully reproduced can survive and flourish.

The problem here, for the religion and science debate, is that religious believers were led to defend an inadequate idea of god (deism) based on an outdated philosophy (Aristotle's concept of final cause and design) in order to support their beliefs. They believed that if the idea of the world as a purposively designed mechanism, pointing to a divine craftsman, was overturned, there would be no further scope for God or religion.

It is therefore important to distinguish between two issues:

1 Is the world 'designed' by some external agency or is it self-designing?
2 Does religious belief depend upon the answer to that first question?

(The assumption between many of the 18th and 19th century debates was that the answer to this second question is that religion does indeed depend upon the world being 'designed'.)

d) Practical science

The 17th and 18th centuries also saw tremendous changes in both technology and in people's attitudes to reason and science. Defoe's *Robinson Crusoe*, published in 1719, presents the castaway as a man who survives through his own inventiveness. The new idea of that era was that nature could be understood and tamed through reason and technology. New instruments were devised – the air pump, telescope, microscope, barometer. **The Royal Society** in England and the **Academie des Sciences** in France were founded in the 17th century, and gave impetus to the emerging sciences. The 18th century saw further technological developments, including the steam engine, the first balloon flight (1783) and gas lighting (1786). In terms of popular perception, these things acted as proof that science, based on observation and reason, must be right because it was able to deliver such practical benefits.

The emergence of new technology was the most visible sign of the tremendous shift in self understanding between the medieval world and people in the 18th century. The world was no longer a place dominated by spiritual forces, influenced by the planetary spheres, with a spiritual end in view. Rather it was a predictable, rational place, a giant mechanism, established by a creator god who did not need to interfere in its workings. This was very much the age of reason, with science as proof of its success.

7 Mathematics

Mathematics provided the background to much of the advancement of science in the 17th and 18th centuries. It is important to recognise the nature of mathematics and the very radical abstraction that it involves.

To put it crudely, you see one person, then another, then another, and as a result you say that there are 'three' people. The concept 'three' is an abstraction from your experience. There is no part of the colour, sound, sight etc. that corresponds to 'three'. Having thus abstracted out from experience the concept of number, those concepts can be manipulated for all sorts of useful purposes. Mathematics, and science based on it, is essentially a way of examining and manipulating these abstract concepts. What Galileo, Descartes or Newton were producing were formulae: ways of predicting; ways of calculating.

Hence, if you say that sound is a set of vibrations in the air, you are abstracting from the experience of sound certain regular patterns that can be quantified and given numerical values. A musical note becomes a frequency that can be given a particular numerical value.

Hence, 'laws of nature' or 'multiplication' are not **things** that exist, they are descriptions of the relationships between abstract concepts that human beings use in order to try to make sense of their experience.

To take a modern example, Stephen Hawking, author of *A Brief History of Time*, is concerned to examine what happened in the very earliest moments of the universe, and does so by examining what happens in the phenomena known as 'black holes'. But he does not need to use a telescope for these investigations, rather he uses mathematics, and is, of course, a Professor of Mathematics. Science, and an understanding of the universe, depends heavily on the manipulation of concepts – and that is where mathematics plays such a central role. Developments in science may be possible as a result of developments in mathematics.

Summary List

Following the rise of modern science, we find religion adopting two conflicting strategies:

● defending traditional philosophy (e.g. the debate over Copernicus / Galileo) or
● setting religion within the new world view (e.g. Newton, Paley, deism).

Essay Questions

1. Critically assess the impact of science upon the Christian religion in the 17th and 18th centuries.
2. To what extent is Locke's distinction between primary and secondary qualities relevant to issues that may divide religion and science?
3. The 17th and 18th centuries saw the triumph of reason over superstition. Do you agree? Give your reasons.

(In answering questions such as these, it is important to distinguish between the Christian religion as such, and the philosophy – from Plato and Aristotle – through which it was being expressed.)

3 Geology and Evolution in the 19th Century

KEYWORDS

natural selection – Darwin's theory that species evolve through the spread and development of those characteristics that help individuals to survive and breed

creationism – the view that species were created as described in Genesis

Social Darwinism – the attempt to examine social behaviour in terms of natural selection

One of the key features of the way in which the world was perceived in medieval times was the balance between that which changed and that which was permanent. Individual creatures were born and died, all particular things known to the senses were subject to change and decay – common mortality. But (following the influence of Plato) the essence of each species was fixed, and these essences (the Platonic 'Forms') defined each individual thing's place and purpose within the universe.

What is more, there was a long tradition – including Augustine, Aquinas, Newton and Paley – of thinkers who saw the wonders of the world as leading the mind naturally to the idea of an intelligent designer and creator: God. God's purpose was revealed in the essence of each species, and just as the flight of the arrow (to use Aquinas' example) made no sense without an archer to shoot it, so the wonderful way in which living things were put together made no sense without a divine designer.

Indeed, until the end of the 18th century, it was commonly believed that the world was less than 6000 years old, that each species had been created separately, and that no species could develop out of another. Such beliefs, which were in line with a literal interpretation of scriptures, were to be challenged by developments within geology and biology during the 19th century. The world was no longer seen as fixed, pre-designed and handed down by a divine creator, but as a process of evolution which, over long periods of time, appeared to be designing itself.

1 Smith & Lyall – the developments in geology

KEY ISSUE
- The implications of geology for the interpretation of Genesis

William Smith (1769–1839), a drainage engineer and amateur geologist, collected information about rock strata and the fossils contained in them. He observed that the deeper strata were older than those nearer the surface, and that the fossils in the strata showed life forms very different from anything found in his own day. He concluded from this that there must have been many successive acts of creation. Geology had become a science capable of revealing history, for Smith's analysis showed successive stages of life on Earth.

Responding to the Biblical account of creation, Smith took the six days referred to in Genesis as six geological periods, rather than literal 24 hour days. He therefore accepted separate acts of creation, but saw them as taking place successively. This view gave rise to a number of 'catastrophe' theories, in which there were a succession of acts of creation, followed by catastrophes, the latest of which had been the flood as described in Genesis.

COMMENT With hindsight, it is interesting that Smith's idea of successive catastrophes and creations, dismissed once a theory of continuous evolution emerged, might come closer to the truth than he realised. We now know that there have been major global extinctions of species – the latest of which, about 65 million years ago, wiped out the dinosaurs – after which the planet's fauna gradually recover.

In his book *Principles of Geology* (published between 1830 and 1833) **Charles Lyell** took a very different view. He argued that the process of geological change was going on all the time, and therefore there was no need to posit separate acts of creation in order to account for the different strata and fossils. This interpretation of change as a continuous process was termed 'uniformitarianism'.

Whether by a series of creations and catastrophes, or a uniform process of change, the new perspective given by 19th century geology did not in itself cause theological problems. It simply required a reinterpretation of the mechanics of creation, and it still allowed for the agency of God in designing and creating species.

It is important to recognise that this successive creation of life forms is not the same thing as evolution. These geological developments were more easily accommodated within traditional beliefs. In *Foot-prints of the Creator*, a book that was very popular when published in 1847, Hugh Miller, a Scottish geologist, argued that the Biblical pattern of creation followed by a fall could be seen throughout the geological record. His point was that species did not improve with the passing of time; rather, as in the Bible, they were created perfect and subsequently 'fell'. It made no sense to argue that humankind developed from earlier life forms, for that would have implied progress, rather than creation and fall.

The key point here was that the idea of humankind developing from other species would, he felt, prevent people from thinking of themselves as spiritual creatures with immortal souls. He therefore separated off his geology from the more controversial ideas about evolution.

Miller's book was published three years after another, more controversial one: Chambers' *The Vestiges of the Natural History of Creation* (1844) had been published anonymously, and spoke of the development and introduction of new species throughout geological time, challenging both the ideas of Biblical creation and also the uniqueness of humankind. But at this stage, Chambers did not have a mechanism with which to explain how such change could come about.

An attempt to reconcile the discoveries of geologists with the account of creation given in Genesis was made by Philip Gosse in *Omphalos* (1857). He asks whether God could have been trying to deceive by creating rocks in the Garden of Eden which contained fossils, or fully grown trees with tree rings, as though they had been growing for years. He concluded that the trees in Eden would have to have had rings, for that is simply what full-grown trees are like. Similarly, Adam would have had a navel – although, clearly, he would not have needed to have one, being created directly by God.

We see in this book, and in other arguments of this time, a struggle to reconcile the growing evidence of a long history of creation with the basic features of the Biblical creation. Some challenged Genesis more directly. A few years earlier (in 1852) Herbert Spencer had argued that if there were indeed no less that 10 million different species that existed or had existed on Earth – which was the more likely: that there had been 10 million individual acts of creation, or that by continual modification and changed circumstances, 10 million different varieties had been produced and were still being produced?

2 Charles Darwin (1809–1882)

KEY ISSUE
- The theory of natural selection as an alternative explanation of 'design'

In spite of the controversy that had been taking place concerning Genesis and the geological record, Darwin's *The Origin of Species* (1859) was hugely controversial because for the first time it suggested a mechanism – natural selection – by which species might develop.

Darwin, the son of a doctor and grandson of Erasmus Darwin (an early evolutionary thinker), studied medicine at Edinburgh and then went to Cambridge, intending to be ordained. In 1831 he was offered a place on board HMS Beagle as a naturalist, in order to explore wildlife in South America. By the time he returned to England in 1836, he was convinced, by the peculiarity of the species he had seen – especially on the Galapagos Islands – and by the way in which some living species were related to fossils, that one species must indeed develop out of another. His task over the next twenty years was to assemble the evidence and develop his theory of how this took place.

The existing theory about changes in species, propounded by Lamark earlier in the century, was that they changed very gradually as a result of the influence of environment and diet. In order for this theory to work, it was essential that characteristics acquired during a lifetime, could be passed on to the next generation (generally known as the 'Theory of Acquired Characteristics'). Darwin first used, but later rejected this theory.

The key to Darwin's work was the theory of **'natural selection'**. This, with hindsight, seems remarkably simple, but it was a radical step. It is simply this:

- within any species there are individual members whose particular characteristics help them to survive better than others
- those who survive to adulthood are able to breed, passing on those characteristics to the next generation
- by this mechanism, with successive generations, those characteristics which improve the chance of survival will be found in an increasing number of individuals within the species, for they will be the ones who survive to breed
- hence the characteristics of a species are gradually modified in favour of those that facilitate survival; thus nature selects those fittest to survive.

In illustrating this theory Darwin pointed out that people had long bred domestic animals for particular characteristics.

In this, he was using a theory about populations and survival produced by Thomas Malthus in *Essays on the Principle of Population* (1798). In this, Malthus had argued that animals and plants produce more offspring than can possibly survive, and that their numbers are controlled by lack of food and/or space. Thus the environment is the limiting factor on the numbers of survivors within any one species. This – given the apparently chance variations in characteristics within a species – provided the mechanism Darwin needed.

This mechanism (now backed up by our understanding of genetics, and therefore the process by which small errors in the copying of genes lead to the chance variations) is very simple. In fact Professor Steve Jones writing in his book *Almost like a Whale* (Doubleday, 1999) describes life as '**a series of successful mistakes**'. That is exactly what evolution is, and it highlights why, as a theory, it is so amazing but also so threatening to those who see God as the designer of everything.

Notice how problematic such a theory could be for religious people. First of all it challenged the unique status of the human species, but even more crucially, it challenged the notion of purpose in creation. Species flourish or decline depending upon their ability to adapt to their environments. There is no externally determined **purpose** in their survival. In other words, the whole of the natural world is based on a process of change that is fundamentally impersonal. That appeared to be contrary to the idea of a god who created the world for a purpose, and whose will is being worked out within it.

a) Was Darwin religious?

When it came to interpreting the Bible, Darwin found that he could not take it literally. In particular he felt that, if God were to act upon the world, he would do it through the operation of natural laws, rather than intervene by way of miracles. He concluded that those of earlier times were more credulous than those of his own day.

In this, he was no different from many people in the 18th and 19th centuries, when – as we saw above – the emphasis was on a rational approach to religion. The fundamental difference between Darwin's position and those of the deists of a century earlier was that he could not have accepted the 'argument from design', since his theory of natural selection took away the need for an external designer.

Darwin retained a belief in God, but was generally agnostic about how the world began. He did, however, express a sense of wonder, that many would see as a form of natural religion. This passage comes from the end of *The Origin of Species*:

> It is interesting to contemplate an entangled bank, clothed with many plants of many kinds, with birds singing on the bushes, with various insects flitting about, and with worms crawling through the damp earth, and to reflect that these elaborately constructed forms, so different from each other, and dependent on each other in so complex a manner, have all been produced by laws acting around us. These laws, taken in the largest sense, being Growth with Reproduction; Inheritance which is almost implied by reproduction; Variability from the indirect and direct action of the external conditions of life, and from use and disuse; a Ratio of Increase so high as to lead to a Struggle for Life, and as a consequence to Natural Selection, entailing Divergence of Character and the Extinction of less-improved forms. Thus, from the war of nature, from famine and death, the most exalted object which we are capable of conceiving, namely the production of the higher animals, directly follows.

And his concluding remark:

> There is grandeur in this view of life, with its several powers having been originally breathed by the Creator into a few forms or into one; and that while this planet has gone cycling on according to the forced law of gravity, from so simple a beginning endless forms most beautiful have been and are being evolved.

Although in many ways this simply sums up the process by which his theory of Natural Selection operates, it also gives a general sense of wonder at the natural order itself.

Whatever one's conclusions about the nature of his religious beliefs, there can be no doubt that, in spite of all the controversies caused by his theory, Darwin was greatly respected, and formed a focus for much of the scientific and intellectual endeavour of his day. He died in 1882 and was buried in Westminster Abbey.

b) Reactions to Darwin

Darwin's theory was supported by Alfred Wallace (who had come independently to similar conclusions about evolution), by the geologist Sir Charles Lyall (see above), by the humanist T H Huxley and others. It was opposed by those who, for religious or other reasons, thought it important to defend the idea of fixed, independently created species.

It is quite wrong to assume that all scientists were for Darwin and all religious people against. Amongst the churchmen who supported him was Charles Kingsley, whose comment – that he considered it as noble a conception of God that he created creatures capable of self-development as to think of God needing to intervene in order to produce new species – was quoted by Darwin in the preface to his second edition. He also had the support of R W Church, Aubrey Moore and F D Maurice, all influential in the Church at that time. It was in any case a time of controversy within the Church of England. *Essays and Reviews*, a collection of seven articles by seven different authors calling for a more liberal approach to religious belief, was published in 1860. Among other things, the debate it stirred up concerned the flexibility with which the Bible should be interpreted – a crucial issue in looking at Genesis in the light of evolution and the findings of geology.

There was, of course, much criticism as well. In a review of *The Origin of Species* in *Quarterly Review* (July 1860), Bishop Wilberforce made the criticism that there was no immediate evidence to show that, even in domesticated animals, there was a change in the species. Mockingly, the review asks: 'Is it credible that all favourable varieties of turnips are intending to become men...?' At the British Association meeting in Oxford in 1860 there was a debate on this between Wilberforce and T H Huxley. Wilberforce asked Huxley whether it was through his grandfather or grandmother that he claimed his descent from an ape.

Not all criticism focused on the religious problems of setting Darwin's theory alongside the account of creation in Genesis. There was also criticism that there appeared to be no direct evidence for transitional states between species within the fossil record itself. This was a serious challenge in terms of science, since it is expected that a theory will be tested out again evidence, and Darwin – although he could show the great variety of species today, and the different forms they took in the past – could not actually show fossil evidence for the sort of gradual process of change that his theory predicted.

Since Darwin's time there have been two general answers to this from within the scientific community. One is that the fossil record is very limited in scope, and the chances of finding a fossil of an intermediate state would be relatively rare – although in recent times more fossil evidence for this is emerging. The other argument is that the process of evolution may not be uniform, but consist in short bursts of change, followed by long periods of stability. This would explain the rarity of intermediate states, simply on a statistical basis.

3 Spencer and Social Darwinism

> **KEY ISSUE**
> ● Spencer explored the implications of Darwin's theory in terms of morality and the organisation of society, coining the term 'survival of the fittest' to introduce the idea that those who were most fit should not be hindered in their progress by the less able

Darwin himself had examined the implications of his theory for human development. In *The Descent of Man* (1871) and *The Expression of the Emotions* (1872) he suggested that human mental ability and social behaviour could be shown to have the same sort of historical development as the human body. This is termed 'Social Darwinism'.

Herbert Spencer used the phrase 'survival of the fittest' to describe the application of the theory of natural selection to ethical and social questions. In this, he went beyond anything Darwin himself had suggested and he was opposed in this by T H Huxley, Darwin's supporter.

The implication of natural selection, according to Spencer, was that human society should follow the struggle for survival in nature. Thus, those not strong enough to live should be allowed to die. He opposed the Poor Laws and state education, since these benefited those least able to take care of themselves. His evolutionary ethic was based on the proposition that whatever makes the totality of life greater, must be good; whatever diminishes life must be bad.

In opposing Spencer, Huxley (and others) put forward the argument that facts about evolution pointed to what **did in fact happen**, but that did not imply that they could be used as a basis for saying what **ought to happen**. This is a crucial point for ethics, where it is generally argued (e.g. by Hume, but later, at the beginning of the 20th century, by G E Moore) that in general you cannot derive an 'ought' from an 'is' – in what is known as the 'naturalistic fallacy'.

In considering Darwin, it is crucially important not to confuse his arguments, or the theory of natural selection, with Spencer's 'survival of the fittest' morality. To do so would be to give the theory implications which Darwin himself did not intend. Whether such morality is implied by Darwin's theory is, of course, a separate matter, but it should not be seen as the only possible interpretation of his work.

In general, it is very dangerous to use Darwin's theory as a justification for social theories. Professor Steve Jones (Daily Telegraph, 16th August 1999) commented:

> Evolution is to the social sciences as statues are to birds; a convenient platform upon which to deposit badly-digested ideas. Biology tells us that we evolved, but when it comes to what makes us human is largely beside the point. There might be inborn drives for rape or for greed, but Homo sapiens, uniquely, need not defer to them. This has not stopped those who try to explain society, from debasing Darwinism to support their creed.

4 Religious responses

KEY ISSUES
- Liberal interpretations of Scripture
- Creationist views, and why they are held

A key religious question in assessing evolution from a Christian point of view (and we need to be clear that this is a matter of Christian doctrinal authority, not a feature of religion in general), is the nature and authority of scripture, and particularly Genesis.

Those who hold that the truth of scripture can only be affirmed if it is interpreted literally, hold that creation must take place over a period of one week in what was (from the geological perspective) the very recent past. Those maintaining this position need to explain the appearance of more ancient life forms, for example within the fossil records. Hence the attempts by Gosse, for example, to stand where Adam stood and see newly made trees complete with rings that gave the impression of age.

A commitment to such a literal interpretation of scripture leads to what is generally termed 'creationism' (see the section below) and it has implications for other aspects of the religion and science debate, notably in the area of miracles.

Those who do not require, as an act of faith, that all scripture should be taken literally, are likely to interpret the scriptural account as a poetic or symbolic way of expressing reality. Hence the argument that the days of creation in Genesis are not to be thought of as periods of 24 hours, but as eras. Thus, like the earlier Book of Scripture / Book of Nature approach of Galileo, Bacon and others, there is the possibility of affirming the essential meaning of Genesis and at the same time allowing the time scale required by evolution.

A second issue is the agency of creation. Kingsley's approach was to see a God who created creatures capable of subsequent development as in no way inferior to a god who needed to intervene for subsequent acts of creation. The parallel here is with the deist view of the creation of the universe, set alongside Newton's laws of physics. At that time, the actual workings of the universe were explained through mechanical laws and did not need the intervention of God, but God still had a place as the originator of the mechanism.

It is crucial here to see exactly what happens to God in these situations: Deism was subsequently regarded by many Christians as an inadequate view of God, because it made him external to the universe, rather than bound up with what happened within it. God was an agent of events only in a very detached and secondary way.

The same issue arises in considering evolution. Should God be considered to be simply the originator of the system that then operates by evolution (Kingsley's argument), or should he be regarded as operating directly through the agency of evolution? **If so, one needs to examine why a god who is regarded as good and loving should use a mechanism which allows progress only at the cost of an almost infinite amount of suffering – for it is only the non-survival to adulthood of a majority that allows a minority to breed and influence the future of the species.**

a) Creationism

The key problems for religion in the theory of natural selection were:

- the concept of 'God' as a creator and designer was made redundant
- the universe appeared to have no purpose, and the direction of evolution was determined by an impersonal mechanism of survival and breeding.

The **creationist** response to evolution was generally based on a literal interpretation of scripture. At the 1925 'Monkey Trial' in Tennessee, John Scopes was prosecuted and fined for teaching evolution, when state law required only the biblical account of creation to be taught in schools (his conviction was later overturned by the State Supreme Court). Even in the 1980s, fundamentalists in

Louisiana campaigned for the biblical account of creation to be given equal emphasis in schools alongside the theory of evolution, and a note in textbooks points out that evolution should be considered a theory rather than a fact. The Catholic Church is more liberal in its approach, since in 1996 the Pope said that evolution could be recognised as 'more than a hypothesis'. Yet in the United States opposition to evolution continues, and in August 1999 the Kansas State Board of Education voted to remove it from the school curriculum. It is estimated that up to 100 million Americans believe that God created humankind very much as it appears today, and did so within the last 10,000 years.

Conservative creationists, holding to a strictly literal interpretation of Genesis, claim that the world was created exactly as described in the Bible. Scientific theories about the age of rocks, for example, are seen as quite irrelevant, on the grounds that God might have planted such evidence for things appearing to have existed long before their actual creation, perhaps in order to test people's faith. This sort of argument dates back to the 19th century, in the early debates about evolution, and includes such questions as whether the trees in the Garden of Eden could have had 'tree rings' (i.e. the appearance of having grown for a number of years in order to reach their mature size), or whether Adam had a navel, and, if so, for what purpose.

Progressive creationists suggest that the world was made as described in Genesis, but that the reference to 'day' in the account did not literally mean a 24 hour period, but was a more general description of each successive period of time. This may allow someone to accept scientific data about the age of the Earth, without thereby being disloyal to the Genesis account.

The key feature of the debate between those who accept the scientific basis of evolution and the creationist, is that of the source of authority. For scientists, authority comes from the impartial analysis of experimental data and the acceptability of a theory by the scientific community. For creationists, ultimate authority comes from the Bible.

COMMENT   Much has happened in biology since the original debates over natural selection, and genetics has shown that species are closely related, sharing genes that perform similar functions in very different bodies. It is amazing that many people today can, in the name of religion, reject such a vast amount of factual evidence. It illustrates the great power that religion can have to overcome reason and common sense, and also the general lack of appreciation of how science works and the methods it uses. The same could be said about the dimensions of the universe – for, looking up on a cloudless night, the stars appear as much fixed in their places today as they did for the medieval star-gazer. Yet we know that the reality of what we see is quite different from what earlier generations could have imagined.

b) The end of religion?

Of course, others responded to the theory of evolution (along with the other scientific advances of the 19th century) very differently. Ernst Haeckel, in *The Riddle of the Universe*, 1899, celebrated the triumphs of science over superstition by taking a materialist view of the universe, in which every aspect of life develops from its material matrix. An account of Haeckel's argument is given in chapter 8 (Freedom and Determinism), since Haeckel's position is one that appears incompatible with freedom as well as with most traditional religious beliefs. He represents one extreme of the 19th century debate, as opposed to the Romantic reaction against what some saw as science's excessive drive to rationalise and formulate abstract theories from experience.

What is clear is that, by the end of the 19th century, there was a feeling – encouraged by the debate over evolution – that religion had, for many thinking people, been replaced by science. It was a view that, early in the 20th century, was to influence the philosophers of the 'Logical Positivist' movement, who saw the success of science as a model for establishing criteria by which they could decide which statements were meaningful and which meaningless. And, of course, the criterion they took was that the meaning of a statement was given in its method of verification. In other words, all meaningful language should be backed by empirical evidence, and without that, language (including most religious language) was meaningless.

A key question for religion is whether it is committed to a dualistic view of reality, with a separate, sacred world. The impact of Darwin's theory was to promote a naturalistic view – that there is one world, not two. As Don Cupitt comments:

> After Darwin we are bound in the end to be committed to a nondualistic view of both the human being and the world.
>
> *After God*, 1997

Summary List

- Geology poses questions about Genesis and the possibility of successive acts of creation
- Natural Selection provides a mechanism to explain the appearance of design
- Some religious responses accept evolution, but retain God's agency
- Creationists reject evolution as contrary to the Bible.

(But note that we shall need to return to some of these issues again, as we consider the New Biology and the genetic basis of the mechanism of evolutionary change.)

Essay Questions

1. To what extent, and in what respects, can it be argued that humankind is unique? Illustrate your answer with reference to Darwin's natural selection theory.

2. Discuss the implication for religious belief of Darwin's theory of natural selection. To what extent is it possible to argue that Darwin was genuinely religious?

3. 'There is grandeur in this view of life...' Do you agree with Darwin that his view of evolution, as set out in *The Origin of Species*, can express the grandeur of a process originated by God?

(There are two aspects to be included here: a) Is evolution inspiring **in itself** and b) Can it inspire as a process 'originated by God'. Does the one detract from the other?)

4. Are there any aspects of the Christian religion that you consider to be rightly threatened by the theory of evolution? If so, what are they, and how might Christianity respond to that threat?

(This question gives the opportunity to mention, and then set aside, those issues for which Christianity appears to have a satisfactory answer, concentrating on any particularly difficult areas.)

4 Sociology and Psychology

Up until the 18th century, religion and science had appeared to offer their own particular interpretations of reality. Sometimes these coincided, sometimes they did not. It was only in the 19th century, however, when science turned its attention to religion and sought to explain it as a human phenomenon.

Thus, as we look at the sciences of Sociology and Psychology, there are two very different things to consider:

- the compatibility of their views with those of religion
- their views on religion itself.

The issue to be debated in the second of these is not whether science can offer explanations which make the religious ones redundant, but whether science can explain the origins and continuing phenomena of religion itself.

1 Marx (1818–1883)

KEY ISSUES
- Alienation as a phenomenon of the proletariat in a capitalist environment
- The illusory benefits offered by religion
- The withering of religion once oppression is removed

The basis of Marx's analysis of human society and the changes that come about within it, is that human survival depends on the supply of food and other goods, and that the production and distribution of these creates a network of social relationships. All other aspects of society (including religion) are shaped by this economic infrastructure.

His analysis of change in society was based on the idea of a 'dialectic' – a central feature of the thinking of the philosopher Hegel – in which one thing (a thesis) produces an opposite reaction (its antithesis) and finally the two are resolved in a synthesis. Marx took this theory and applied it to the material base of society. His 'dialectical materialism' saw social change mainly in terms of the conflict between classes.

One feature of the capitalist society, according to Marx, is that working people suffer from 'alienation' from nature, from their true selves and from one another. This was caused because they were required to work within a structure which detached them from the end product of their labours, and made them simply part of an impersonal capitalist enterprise.

His concern was to analyse society, criticise elements that led to alienation, and thereby encourage people – particularly the working class or proletariat – to take steps to overcome alienation and to free themselves from all that repressed them.

a) The Marxist critique of religion

Marx believed that religion encouraged alienation, because it offered illusory, spiritual goals, which were held out by way of compensation to those who were suffering. These spiritual goals, he believed, took from people the incentive to do something here and now to improve their situation.

As such, religion was encouraged by those in power as a means of control. The spiritual rewards on offer provided an alternative to the material benefits that might have been theirs through revolution. Thus religion became a dangerous substitute for real progress:

> Religion is the sigh of the oppressed creature, the heart of a heartless world, the soul of the soulless environment. It is the opium of the people.

> (from *Introduction to the Critique of Hegel's Philosophy of Law*)

If religion survived through the longing of those who were oppressed, Marx argued that it would not be overthrown by arguing for atheism, but by creating a social revolution that would enable people to take responsibility for their own welfare. Remove the causes of oppression, and religion would no longer be needed and would therefore wither.

Several key features emerge from this analysis:

- Religion is not neutral within society. It plays a part in the social structure within which it is practised, and its continuance may depend on that social structure rather than any truths that it may propound.
- As he saw it, religion had a negative and compensatory role, making it of service only to those who were being oppressed. This may have

reflected the situation of his day; it is a matter of debate whether that is a universal feature of religion.

- With social revolution and the achievement of real goals, he believed that religion would become unnecessary and wither away.
- In examining any phenomenon, science looks at what causes it and what maintains it. In a sense, Marx did that in terms of the needs of both the working classes (their longing) and those who oppress them (maintaining control by offering religion's substitute satisfactions).
- Notice particularly that Marx is not concerned with the **truth** of religion, but with the **function** of religion.
- Marx saw religion as a force opposing change. He had no concept of religion as a means of encouraging social justice.

Such social analysis, although very different from physics or biology, is a genuine form of science. Science is based on looking at phenomena and formulating hypotheses about them, which may be confirmed by further examination and experiment. That is precisely what Marx was doing, and his theories are to be accepted or rejected depending on the extent to which they are successful in continuing to explain religion.

One criticism, for example, is that many religious groups promote social action. How can they be accommodated in his theory? Another major criticism is that, with the emancipation of the proletariat, religion has not withered; therefore it must serve a function other than to offer illusory, substitute goals.

One may therefore wish to see Marx as offering a valid set of theories for the particular social and religious situation of his day, but not as having produced a theory of universal relevance. (This is not unusual in science – in the light of relativity, Newtonian physics is seen as valid only within a narrow set of parameters.)

2 Durkheim (1858–1917)

KEY ISSUE
- Religion as a vehicle of social cohesion

In *The Elementary Forms of Religious Life*, Durkheim argued that religion provided a framework of thought which was able to hold together the ideas and values that are shared by a society. Religion depends on there being a community of people who practise it, it is not about detached ideas and speculations. Particular religious beliefs may change, but the fundamental need for some sort of religion remains:

> There can be no society which does not feel the need of upholding and reaffirming at regular intervals the collective ideas which make its unity and its personality.

For Durkheim, religion performs the function of integrating and strengthening the group of people who practise it. Something becomes sacred because it is the means by which a group of people come to an overall understanding of themselves and their world. Thus for Durkheim, the real object of religious veneration is not a god, but society itself – for society, and its need for cohesion, is what lies behind religion.

Most sociologists today would agree with Durkheim that religion can express the values of society, and therefore that defending a particular religion is also a sign of social identity, but they would not try to go beyond that to say that society itself was in any way sacred.

3 Weber (1864–1920)

KEY ISSUE
● Religion as an inspiration and agent of social change

Two features of Weber's sociology are of particular interest:

1 He emphasises the 'charisma' of religious leaders, who inspire their followers and pass on something of their own powers to them. Thus, in contrast to Durkheim, whose analysis of religion saw it primarily as a function of society as a whole, Weber saw it as a reflection of the potential and inspiration of individuals.

2 He also took the important step of recognising that, in the relationship between religion and society, it was not just that society influenced religion, but that religion influenced society. So, for example, the Protestant ethic of hard work and personal frugality (as promoted particularly in Calvinism) contributed to the rise and success of capitalism.

Notice how this contrasts with Marx. For Marx it is the economic and social structures that give rise to and shape religion. For Weber, religion has an active part to play in the shaping of society.

Other sociologists have contributed views on the place of religion. **Malinowski** described the way in which religion deals with situations of emotional stress and trauma. **Berger and Luckmann** show the way in which it contributes to the overall framework of understanding and self understanding, without which a society cannot hold together. **Simmel** examined acts of selfless devotion (e.g. of a parent for a child, or of a patriot for his or her nation) and showed the way in which these paralleled religious devotion. He thus saw these features of religion as universal human traits, without which society could not survive.

In general it is important to see that for sociologists what matters is how religion functions within society, not the truth content of religious beliefs.

> **NOTE** This section does no more than touch on some of the classical sociological theories of religion. *Religion* in the parallel *Access to Sociology* series gives a broad overview of the Sociology of Religion.

4 Freud

> **KEY ISSUES**
> * Religion as an obsessional neurosis
> * *The Future of an Illusion* – his prognosis for religion

Jewish by birth, but not practising his religion, Freud spent most of his life in Vienna. After training in medicine, he worked as a hospital doctor, taking a particular interest in neuro-pathology and in the effects of the drug cocaine. He then set up in private practice, dealing with nervous conditions, especially hysteria, and developed a method of treatment called psychoanalysis. In this, through the analysis of dreams and by the free association of thoughts, a person could be led to articulate tensions which were previously locked within the unconscious mind, but which manifested in terms of bizarre behaviour or nervous or morbid mental states.

Freud is relevant to the study of religion and science for at least three reasons:

1 His theory about the unconscious mind raises questions about human nature, about whether we are actually free to choose what to think or feel, and about the image of God as father and creator. According to Freud, the mind is divided into the conscious (the part of which we are aware) the pre-conscious (including those things that we may not be aware of at this moment, but which we are capable of remembering), and the unconscious (which most importantly includes the memories of events which we are unable to remember, generally because they are too painful or embarrassing, especially events that took place in the earliest years of life, and which have therefore been repressed). Actions which a person may believe to be a matter of conscious choice may in fact be determined by unconscious influences, over which he or she has no control.

2 He claimed to give a scientific explanation of those personal aspects of life – motives, fears, hopes – which are seen as immediately relevant to the practice of religion.
3 He describes religion as an illusion, and offers a reductionist interpretation of its origins and continuing appeal. In other words, religion could be portrayed as a projection of realities that are actually to be found within the unconscious, which would tend to diminish its objective reality, whilst explaining its power over individuals and society.

Freud saw each stage of life as producing tensions. If these were not faced and resolved at the time, they could become buried in the unconscious, to re-appear later in life to create emotional or behavioural problems. He was particularly interested in neuroses which involved compulsive tidying routines or excessive washing. He ascribed these to feelings of uncleanness instilled in childhood. The adult is actually clean, but still feels dirty and therefore needs to wash. Such behaviour he called an 'obsessional neurosis'.

Freud claimed that such neuroses could be cured if the sufferer was able to discover the root of the problem within his or her unconscious mind, as a result of which the tensions can be acknowledged and resolved. In other words, once a person sees that their feelings of dirtiness come from childhood and do not relate to their present state, they may be freed from their compulsive behaviour.

Freud saw, in the meticulous observations of religious rites and duties, a form of activity similar to the compulsive behaviour of his neurotic patients. He therefore believed religion to be a '**universal obsessional neurosis**', motivated by unconscious guilt.

In *The Future of an Illusion* (1927) he set out various benefits of religion:

- that the threat from the impersonal forces of nature is handled by seeing them as controlled by a God; in other words, it comforts, by suggesting that whatever happens is the will of a loving God
- that God takes the place of a human father, giving the adult the protection that a child looks for
- that the believer hopes to influence events through the help of God, who rules the world
- that there is a sense of dignity from having a relationship with God
- that religion offers teaching that seeks to overcome the perceived threat of death
- that religion gives a convenient explanation of otherwise inexplicable events.

But, these he sets against the following arguments:

- that faith is actually an illusion, based on what people would like to be true, rather than what is actually the case

- that divine rules and regulations may go against ordinary personal needs, thereby limiting personal growth.

There are many other interesting areas of Freud's analysis of religion, including his views on its origins, but for the purpose of the religion and science issues there are two crucial points to be made:

1 Freud showed that the motive for holding a religious belief may spring from personal and emotional need. Freud called religion an 'illusion' because he saw it as a projection of unconscious needs. On the other hand, it is important to recognise that this does not actually claim that religious beliefs are incorrect, i.e. God may exist, even if the reason for wanting to believe in him is the desire for a substitute father. So although Freud's argument may tend to undermine religious belief, it does not actually disprove it.

2 Crucial also for religion and science was Freud's claim that our actions are controlled by the unconscious mind. For him, beliefs and attitudes are not freely or rationally chosen, but are determined by experiences in our early childhood, buried in our unconscious. Again, this does not in itself refute any particular religious beliefs or moral convictions, but it tends to undermine any attempt to give them a metaphysical basis. They are, for Freud, a product of our unconscious mind.

The implication of Freud's position here is that, if religion is promoted because it fulfils emotional and psychological needs, then the balanced and emotionally secure person does not need religion. This is, of course, similar to Marx's idea that, once people recognise that their needs can be met in this life, they will not accept a substitute happiness in a future one.

5 Jung (1875–1961)

KEY ISSUES
- The collective unconscious
- The Archetypes
- The positive psychological role for religion

Unlike Freud, who saw religion as an illusion hindering personal development, Jung gave it an important and positive role in human life. He claimed that all those people over the age of thirty five who came to him with their problems were suffering from what finally amounted to a loss of the religious view of life. He remained agnostic about religious beliefs, whilst holding that religion itself had a positive part to play in human life. He accepted (following Feuerbach and Marx) that religious images were projections of the self, but then sought to show the importance that such projections could have in terms of the spiritual enrichment of human life.

a) The collective unconscious

Jung introduced the idea of the collective unconscious. In this, an individual shares in a cluster of images (**archetypes**) found in different cultures and ages. Religion provided a rich source of these images, through which an individual is enabled to share in the cultural life of the whole race, and through which he or she can achieve a sense of personal integrity.

As a scientist, Jung did not argue about whether or not God existed. He held that a person's knowledge is limited to those things which are experienced. His concern was to examine the idea of God in the mind of the believer and see how it worked. He also wanted to show that such ideas were found in all eras and cultures, and that they could have a positive, integrating effect.

Two important points need to be kept in mind in assessing psychological or sociological theories of religion:

1 They reflect the experience of religion at a particular time and in a particular culture. In other words, if Freud's view of religion is one in which people are obsessed with guilt and forgiveness, his theories apply particularly to that aspect of religion. Such theories cannot apply to a religion like Buddhism, which includes neither guilt nor the concept of a 'father figure' god. Like all scientific hypotheses, they apply to a limited range of experience, and are open to revision.

2 They are a reminder that religion is not just a set of philosophical propositions, but a living experience. Psychological and sociological factors play a part in formulating and maintaining religious beliefs. The theories of Freud or Marx would suggest that those who do not have irrational feelings of guilt and unworthiness, or who do not look to an afterlife to compensate them for present suffering because they are in fact rather enjoying life just as it is, are less likely to be attracted by what religion has to offer. Whether that is in fact the case cannot be determined by a philosophical argument, but by observation of the actual pattern of religious belief in society today.

Summary List

- Marx sees religion as offering illusory, spiritual goals to those who suffer, thereby encouraging alienation and discouraging social revolution
- Durkheim points out that religion aids and expresses social cohesion

- Weber sees individual inspiration and social vision through religion
- Freud considers religion a universal obsessional neurosis
- Jung points to a positive role for religion in aiding personal integrity and social integration

Essay Questions

1.

[Many people] find it especially difficult to accept the objective or metaphysical side of religion, the side that postulates and describes various supernatural beings, powers and events. Though in many ways such beliefs are imaginatively attractive, we have little or no reason to think them true; they evidently belong to a bygone age, and they invite us back into a childhood world. The universe becomes again a vast family home in which we are destined to remain in perpetuity, members of the younger generation under benevolent supervision.

Yet although the doctrinal side of religion may thus seem hard to stomach and hard to credit, few people are happy to be quite without any religious dimension to their lives. At least they would like to retain something of a religious sense of life's meaning and something of religious ritual, values and spirituality.

From the opening of *Taking Leave of God* by Don Cupitt, 1980

Comment on this quotation from the standpoint of Freud and then of Jung, taking care to distinguish between them.

2. In what ways might sociologists explain people's continuing need for religion, as described by Cupitt in the passage given above?

3. Do you consider the beliefs and attitudes of the Christian religion to be healthy from a personal and social point of view?

(In answering this question, you will need to define what you mean by 'health' in a personal and a social context.)

5 Twentieth Century Developments

1 The New Physics

KEY ISSUES
- Newtonian physics is shown to be correct only within certain very limited parameters
- Relativity theory introduces the interconnected nature of space, time, mass and energy
- Quantum theory introduces the idea of unpredictability at the level of particle physics, and of the intrusive nature of investigation (we influence by observing)

a) Relativity

Einstein formulated two theories of relativity. The first (in 1905) is termed 'Special Relativity'. This is summarised in the formula $E=mc^2$, linking mass and energy. Since E stands for energy, m for mass and c for the speed of light, the formula shows that a very small mass is equivalent to a very large amount of energy.

The second, termed 'General Relativity', followed in 1916, and relates time, space, mass and energy. Through the influence of gravity, both space and time may be changed. Thus, for example, time passes more slowly where there is less gravity, and space is also elastic, being compressed as gravity increases. But gravity is related to mass – since the larger the mass of a body, the greater its gravitational pull – and mass (according the Special Relativity) is related to energy.

There are two key things to appreciate about the significance of this for religion and science issues:

- Relativity encourages a 'holistic' approach to understanding the universe. Einstein's theories were a major step in the direction of finding a single theory to explain everything. Relativity shows that everything is interconnected.

• Relativity did not show Newtonian physics to be wrong; rather it showed that it described laws that operated within a very localised and limited set of conditions. If you consider space, time, gravity and mass as they appear to an observer on the earth's surface, then Newtonian physics works well. On the other hand, once you start to look at the extremes of the universe, gravity starts to warp both space and time, and the Newtonian perspective is of little use.

Since Einstein's day, great progress has been made in working towards 'theories of everything'; the goal of finding the most fundamental principles which will link all the basic forces in the universe, showing how they have developed and therefore exactly how they relate to one another. Relativity was the first step in the direction towards such an overall theory.

b) Quantum theory

The idea that matter comprises atoms separated from one another by empty space, is not new; it was a view put forward by the Greek Atomist philosophers Leucippus and Democritus in the 5th century BCE (see above page 6).

A major new development came about early in the 20th century, with the recognition (following a discovery made by Max Plank in 1901) that radiation (e.g. light, or energy) was seen as coming not in a continuous stream but in little packets, or 'quanta' – hence the term 'quantum theory'.

Until the discovery of the electron in 1897, the atom was thought to be indivisible, and was visualised as a very small but solid portion of physical matter. The atom was then found to have a nucleus comprising protons and neutrons, with electrons circling round it, like planets in a solar system. It was insubstantial; mostly empty space.

Particle physics (the term used for the study of sub-atomic particles) developed from that point, with atoms recognised as made up of many different particles, some divisible into smaller 'quarks', which themselves come in different forms. Matter is therefore far from simple. It is composed of complex arrangements of nuclear forces, binding together particles, which themselves cannot always be distinguished as independent entities.

Aristotle had made a distinction between the material cause of something and its formal cause. We think of something having a particular form and made out of a substance:

But when we come to the ultimate particles constituting matter, there seems to be no point in thinking of them as consisting of some material. They are, as it were pure shape, nothing but shape; what turns up again and again in successive observations is this shape, not an individual speck of material.

E Schrodinger *Science and Humanism*, CUP, 1952, p21

Of course, shape here does not refer to geometric shape – particles are far too small to be thought of in that way. The shape here is the patterns that give evidence for that particle. This is quite a difficult concept to grasp, but is essential to an understanding of modern physics. The pictures or models we use to describe things cannot be 'true' (since we cannot compare the picture with the original to see if it fits), rather we can describe it as 'adequate'. A model is adequate if it can be used successfully in predictions.

Take the example of iron. When a small amount of iron is set within an electric arc, it heats up to a very high temperature, and the iron vapour gives off a distinctive spectrum of light (which shows up as tens of thousands of individual lines in the spectrum pattern). That spectrum pattern is always the same, wherever iron is found. Thus even if we cannot see iron atoms, we know if iron is present by observing the spectrum of light. Thus it is possible to tell what distant stars are made of, simply by analysing the spectral patterns of the light they emit. (NB When a lump of iron is heated, it glows, but the light emitted at that temperature is continuous across the spectrum. This is because the individual iron atoms are close together, and interfere with one another, thus blurring the individual lines of the spectrum. It is only at extremely high temperatures that the distinctive lines emerge.)

Particles seem to change, depending upon how they are observed, and at this level their behaviour appears to be random (unlike the predictable laws of Newtonian physics). This leads to an important feature of Quantum theory that is sometimes misunderstood and can cloud the associated religion and science issues. **Quantum theory cannot predict the action of individual particles, but describes the atomic world in terms of probabilities, based on the observation of very large numbers**. (This is rather like an opinion poll, which can predict how a population will vote, but is unable to be precise about the way in which any one person will do so.) There arose a debate between Niels Bohr, a quantum physicist who held that such uncertainty was inherent in nature, and Einstein, who rejected the idea of random happenings – declaring 'God does not play dice.'

In 1927, Heisenberg, pointed out that, in an experiment, the more accurately the position of an atom is measured, the more difficult it is to predict its velocity (and vice versa). It is impossible to know both things at once. The crucial debate here – as highlighted by Einstein's original objection – is whether such uncertainty is caused by the way in which we examine nature, or whether it belongs to nature itself. In other words, is it just that we have not developed the right technique for the simultaneous measuring of the speed and position of an atom, or is it that the atom is not something of which it is theoretically possible to specify speed and position? This is an important consideration for the religion and science debate, highlighting once again the way in which our understanding of the world may be coloured by the very means by which we can come to know it.

It also has implications for the freedom and determinism debate (see page 80). Laplace had argued that, in theory, everything in the universe can be predicted from a knowledge of the present: quantum theory denies this. However, it should be remembered that this indeterminacy applies only to this atomic and sub-atomic level of reality. Once we start to deal with larger objects, Newtonian physics can be used. Hence, it is unwise to cite Heisenberg as a scientific support for a theory which claims that, for example, the actions of human beings cannot, in theory, be predicted.

In all this, it also becomes clear that there is a totally new relationship between observer and observed. The world cannot be divided between independent, objective things and human observers. **Whatever we observe, we influence.** The Quantum physicists Bohr and Heisenberg made this clear, with the implication that an object has no existence independent of our observation of it. We cannot get 'outside' our process of observation to see what is 'really' there – it makes no sense to think in those terms.

This, again, is not a new debate. In Ancient Greece, Protagoras argued that all we know are the sensations we receive, whilst Democritus argued for 'things' that existed independent of our sensations.

2 The new biology

KEY ISSUE
* The form of all living things is determined by the chemical sequence, sections of which are called genes, strung out along DNA molecules. This provides both the information for individual development, and the random mutations that drive natural selection

Discoveries in the 1950s led to a study of biology at the molecular level, where it seemed to follow the laws of physics. It was popularly believed that biology could simply be reduced to physics – in other words, that the bodies of living things could be understood by reducing them to their individual molecules, each obeying physical laws.

Against this it was argued (e.g. by A R Peacocke and P Davies) that physics and chemistry cannot give a full account of living things (i.e. that the human body may be made up of water and other chemicals, but these do not define what it is to be human, nor can the laws under which their molecules operate give much of a guide to how the whole human being operates.) Biological life is far more complex than the molecules of which it is comprised, therefore different concepts are needed for each level of complexity. Living things can no more be described in terms of individual cells, than a painting can be appreciated by analysing threads of canvas or brush-strokes of paint.

The discovery of **Deoxyribonucleic Acid (DNA)** in 1953 provided the basis for modern molecular biology. All living things are formed out of chemical substances (waters, sugars, fats etc.). Of these, the nucleic acids (RNA and DNA) and proteins control the way in which living cells are put together. **Proteins** are made up of **amino acids**, whose production depends on information provided by DNA. In the nucleus of each cell (except for sperm, egg and red blood cells) are 23 pairs of **chromosomes**, which contain the DNA, made up of two strands of chemical units called **nucleotides**, spiralled into a double helix. Information contained in the sequence of nucleotides (sections of which are called **genes**) determines how the protein is made. **Thus, every cell (of which the human body has about 30 trillion!) contains the information needed to reproduce every other cell in the body.**

NOTE One practical use of such information is in forensic identification. Since the genetic code is unique to each person, but contained in every cell of his or her body, it is possible to identify someone from a small sample of cells from any part of their body (e.g. small quantities of blood or hair from the scene of a crime). The genetic analysis of the sample from the crime scene can be compared with that of the suspect.

The term 'genetic' is used for the information contained in the DNA, which determines the character of every organism. A **mutation** takes place when one of the amino acids in a protein chain is changed for another. If a mutation takes place in a germ cell, which is rare, it can be passed on to children; mostly they occur in non-germ cells, and lead to an irregular growth in cell tissue. 'Mistakes' are rare, because the chromosomes work in pairs, and a good copy from one usually dominates a defective copy from the other.

A medical application
Within the human body, living cells are being produced all the time, controlled by the genetic information. When a mistake occurs, the body normally detects that this has happened, and the cell is destroyed. If, for some reason, the body's immune mechanism fails to detect the error, the cell may grow and reproduce out of control, forming a cancer. At the moment this is treated by removing the malignant cells by surgery, or progressively reducing the cancer by causing a level of damage to all cells, on the assumption that the healthy ones are better able to recover than the malignant ones. The gene that produces the protein that inhibits the growth of malignant cells has been identified. It is hoped that this will eventually lead to a cure for cancer, by giving patients exactly the right gene proteins to enable their bodies to reject and eliminate the malignant cells.

Darwin's theory of natural selection showed how, given a number of variations within individuals in a species, those with particular advantages would survive, breed and influence the process of change in that species. What Darwin did not know was the reason for the random occurrence of varieties, some useful, some not. We now know that the reason for variety is that the genetic code is not always copied exactly, leading to the occasional mutations, some of which survive and reproduce because they work well alongside the rest of the genes in the 'gene pool' of that particular species.

There is also a fundamental similarity at the molecular level between all forms of life. The building blocks of the genetic code are universal, and the genetic difference between species is often quite small. At one time, the evidence for evolution depended on the fossil record; nowadays it also comes from genetics. Certain genes play very similar roles in different species, and this suggests that, if you trace those species back, you will come to a common ancestor, from which each has inherited its particular genetic material. Along with the mechanism of natural selection, it shows just how interconnected and similar all life is.

a) Some religious implications of the new biology

In order to appreciate the force of the challenge to the traditional concept of a designer god posed by modern concepts of biology, it is important to step back and consider the traditional argument for the existence of God based on design (see, for example, Paley's argument about the watch and the watchmaker on page 25).

The idea of nature being wonderfully designed by God finds expression in the poetry of Wordsworth. In *Tintern Abbey* he wrote:

... and I have felt
A presence that disturbs me with the joy
Of elevated thoughts: a sense sublime
Of something far more deeply interfused.
Whose dwelling is the light of setting suns,
And the round ocean and the living air,
And the blue sky, and in the mind of man;
A motion and a spirit, that impels
All thinking things, all objects of all thought,
And rolls through all things...

Now it might be argued that such a sense of the presence of a spiritual power underlying everything is essential to religion. On the other hand, is it essential for such a belief that the being is a rational designer, evidenced by the way in which everything works together? Does it make any significant difference to the argument if the agency of the design is natural selection?

One of the most persuasive exponents of the implications of the new biology and the new perspective it gives us on evolution is Richard Dawkins. In his best-selling book *The Blind Watchmaker*, he examines the way in which more and more complex organisms can be formed by the application of one or two quite simple principles. The force of his argument is that you do not have to have some **external** source of rationality or design in order to explain evolution. This he further developed in *Climbing Mount Improbable*, where, what looks an impossible feat of design becomes quite inevitable, given sufficient time and sufficient numbers.

Thus the natural feature of life to self-organise and the inevitability of the rise of more and more complex forms over a period of time, is linked directly with the genetic basis of life. Our uniqueness and our 'design' is given through the very complex genetic code that determines how every cell in our body is to develop.

The genetic basis of evolution is sometimes presented as though the whole process was random, thus denying any sense of direction. This is not correct. **The gene mutations that arise do so at random, but once those mutations have appeared, some succeed and some do not. In other words, there is a self-selection process that operates, depending on the ability of that particular mutation to survive in its environment.** The process of natural selection, as set out by Darwin, is not made entirely redundant by the introduction of genetic theory. Genetics shows the process by which chances are thrown up, some of which are taken and some of which are lost.

Another book by Richard Dawkins, *The Selfish Gene*, illustrated a further implication of the genetic basis of evolution, and one that has immediate implications for ethical and religious views. According to Dawkins, our genes are inherently 'selfish', not in some morally pejorative sense, but simply that their task is to promote survival and successful reproduction. The human bodies through which they operate can therefore be thought of as their 'survival suits'.

What you cannot do (and Dawkins has made this quite clear) is somehow take the imagery too literally (individual genes cannot be, in a literal sense, 'selfish' – for that applies at the very different level of patterns of human behaviour), nor should one move from biological theory to social theorising (e.g. as Spencer did on the basis of Darwin). Thus Dawkins is **not** saying that genetic theory justifies 'selfish' behaviour on the human level: a misunderstanding arising out of the title of his book.

It is important to get an imaginative grasp on the immensity of new information revealed by genetics. Consider human development from conception to birth. Gradually, from a fertilised egg and then a tiny cluster of cells, the material differentiates, the organs form, and a human being slowly takes shape. That development is an amazing process, ascribable, from a religious point of view, to a divine designer and creator. Yet we know that the fertilised egg actually contains all the genetic information to produce that unique human being. What is more, the information that programs that development shows parallels with the information that will go to produce countless other species. Life is a matter of three million bits of information, stored on the DNA's double helix; the purpose of most of it is yet unknown, but within it are the 70,000 genes which contain all the instructions for building a human being.

NOTE   There are other broad areas of scientific theory that are relevant to the interface between religion and science. These include, for example, theories about chaos or complexity. The first of these examines the way in which very small and unpredictable occurrences in one place may trigger a sudden and dramatic change in another. The second looks at the way in which nature has a tendency to self-produce more and more complex organisms by the application of a few basic rules.

There is also the issue about the Second Law of Thermodynamics (which points out that in every process there is some loss of energy and heat, and that all things are therefore gradually tending towards a cooler, less organised state) and how this might be applied to the universe as a whole. Along with this is the consideration of the difference between closed systems, which gradually wind down as their energy is dissipated, and open systems (like human beings), which have the capacity to take into themselves energy from outside, and can therefore self-sustain, grow and become more complex.

These cannot be examined in any detail here; however the way in which religion relates to such theories is not essentially different from its response to the broad developments in physics and biology that we have already outlined.

Summary List

- Relativity and quantum theory show the limitations of earlier Newtonian physics
- Genetics shows the information base for all living things, and shows the mechanism of random mutation upon which the process of natural selection leads to the evolution of species
- The information-rich basis of genetics challenges the traditional idea of design as being imposed on nature by a divine creator

Essay Questions

1. Relativity and quantum theory, by broadening the horizons of physics once set by Newton, require a believer to take a correspondingly broader concept of God. Discuss.

   (A question such as this invites a critical examination of the narrow 'deism' suggested by the Newtonian world-view. Essentially, it invites an imaginative approach to the concept of 'God' within a world–view that takes relativity and quantum theory into account.)

2. Discuss the religious implications of the fact that humankind shares many of its genes with other species.

   (Consider the challenge posed to the traditional religious affirmation of the uniqueness of humankind. This also has religious and ethical implications for the treatment of other species and the environment by humans.)

6 The Methods of Science and Religion

KEYWORDS

rationalism – the view that all claims to knowledge should be based on, and assessed by, human reason

empiricism – the view that all knowledge starts with sense experience

deduction – the process of working out of the logical implication of a general principle

induction – arriving at an hypotheses through examining evidence and testing it through experiments

model – an image, taken from common experience, used in order to explain a phenomenon

paradigm – an example of established scientific work, used as the basis for further developments in the subject

'Method' refers to the process by which beliefs are established, and the grounds upon which they may be defended.

> ... it is not *what* a man of science believes that distinguishes him, but *how* and *why* he believes it. His beliefs are tentative, not dogmatic; they are based on evidence, not on authority or intuition.
>
> Bertrand Russell *The History of Western Philosophy*

1 Background

Historically, the foundation of the modern scientific method required three things:

1 a trust in evidence and experiment as a means of acquiring knowledge
2 a desire to challenge and evaluate all claims to truth, setting aside the authority of both the Church and Aristotle
3 a belief that the world is both orderly and intelligible.

Bacon (1561–1626), Newton (1642–1727) and others insisted that knowledge started with observation, from which reason could deduce the laws of nature, expressing them in mathematical terms. This is rational *empiricism* (for the claim that all knowledge comes from experience see also Hume on miracles, page 92).

By contrast, **Descartes (1596–1650)**, often described as the founder of modern philosophy, used the method of systematic doubt in order to establish what could be known for certain. Since the senses can sometimes deceive us (e.g. when mistaking a dream for reality) he doubted all empirical evidence. His only certain knowledge was of himself as a thinking being ('I think therefore I am.') since to deny it would involve self-contradiction. This approach, seeing the mind, rather than the senses, as the starting point for knowledge, is termed *rationalism*.

Generally speaking, the method that has dominated the world of science from the 16th to the 20th century has been based on empiricism, rather than rationalism. In other words, it has started with observation and experiment, rather than with pure thought. In terms of 20th century science, however, this needs to be qualified, since it has become increasingly clear that our understanding of the world depends upon the way in which we think and interpret the information that comes through the senses.

2 Deduction and induction

There are two fundamentally different processes involved in gaining knowledge: deduction and induction.

a) The deductive approach

If you know one mathematical equation, you can deduce others from it; if you know the rules by which a game is played, you can deduce what individual moves are likely to be made. There is nothing wrong with the deductive method as such: provided you know the rules are correct and that they apply to this particular situation, various things can be deduced that are perfectly valid. You do not have to conduct experiments to know that $2 + 2 = 4$ in each and every case, it is known to be true by definition.

Sometimes, however, what is deduced does not square with what is experienced – we do not see what reason tells us we should see. In such cases, we need to look at the assumptions upon which the deduction is based. We have already seen in the historical section above (pages 13–15) that the medieval view of the heavens was that they were perfect, and therefore that the planets had to move in circles, since the circle was a perfect shape. This piece of deduction conflicted with evidence, and therefore the underlying assumption (the perfection of the heavens) was challenged.

b) The inductive approach

The inductive method, as used by science, works in this way:

- observe and gather data (evidence; information) seeking to eliminate, as far as possible, all irrelevant factors
- analyse your data and draw conclusions from it in the form of hypotheses
- devise experiments to test out those hypotheses i.e. if this hypothesis is correct then certain experimental results should be anticipated
- modify your hypothesis, if necessary, in light of the experiments
- from the experiments, the data and the hypotheses, argue for a theory (this is the crucial stage in the inductive part of scientific method)
- once you have a theory you can – using deduction – predict things that should be the case if your theory is correct
- establish tests which can either verify or disprove the theory.

It is clear that this process of induction, by which a theory is arrived at by the analysis and testing out of observed data, can yield at most only a high degree of probability. There is always the chance that an additional piece of information will show that the original hypothesis is wrong, or that it only applies within a limited field. The hypothesis, and the scientific theory that comes from it, is therefore open to modification.

Theories that are tested out in this way lead to the framing of scientific laws. Now it is important to establish exactly what is meant by 'law' in this case. In common parlance, 'law' is taken to be something which is imposed, a rule that is to be obeyed. But it would be wrong to assume that a scientific law can dictate how things behave. **The law simply describes behaviour, it does not control it.** If something behaves differently, it is not to be blamed for going against a law of nature, it is simply that either:

- there is an unknown factor that has influenced this particular situation and therefore modified what was expected, or
- the law of nature is inadequately framed, and needs to be modified in order to take this new situation into account.

Generally speaking, an activity is called 'scientific' if it follows the inductive method. On these grounds, the work of Marx could be called scientific in that he based his theories on accounts of political changes in the societies he studied. Similarly, a behavioural psychologist can claim to be scientific on the basis of the methods used – observing and recording the responses of people and animals to particular stimuli, for example.

In evaluating what counts as science, method counts for more than subject matter. Thus, for example, astronomy is regarded as a science; astrology is not. This is because the former is based on observable facts, whilst the latter is based on a mythological scheme.

3 Evidence and objectivity

KEY ISSUES

● That progress is made in science when theories are challenged and modified
● That science cannot eliminate the influence of theory in the way it selects and presents evidence

---

Karl Popper (1902–1994), in his book *The Logic of Scientific Discovery* (1934, trans.1959), makes the important point that science seeks theories that are both logically self-consistent, and that can be **falsified**. It is curious to think of science as a process by which existing theories are falsified, but that is the implication of Popper's view. The reason lies in the method by which that theory has been reached in the first place. A scientific theory goes beyond what can be experienced. It takes all the available evidence, and on the basis of that, frames a general hypothesis – a hypothesis which should, if it is correct, account for other situations for which we do not have evidence at present. Now it is possible to go on collecting more and more data to illustrate the truth of the theory. The more evidence we have, the more likely it is that the theory is correct. We can never absolutely **prove** that a theory is true by this method – all we can show is that it continues to account for the evidence.

Science makes progress, however, once a theory is shown to be false or in need of modification. In other words, a scientist comes up against evidence that does not fit the theory, and consequently the theory has to be modified in order to take the new evidence into account. A scientific theory is therefore accepted on a provisional basis until such time as it is falsified.

This leads Popper to say that a scientific theory **cannot be compatible with all the logically possible evidence. If a theory claims that it can never be falsified, then it is not scientific.** For science, it is important to have statements that contain real information; but the more information it has, the more likely it is to be proved incorrect. This is its strength, not its weakness, for if you find a statement with the maximum probability of being true, it will contain minimal information. For example, I may say 'The Sun will rise tomorrow.' This has a maximum probability of being true, but it will hardly cause any excitement, nor revolutionise people's views. On the other hand, if I say 'It will start raining at 6.47am tomorrow', that information might be quite important, but has a high probability of being false – and is certainly not going to be true for all locations! **The ideal for science is to be able to make statements with the maximum amount of information that is compatible with a real possibility of that information being correct.**

At one time science's attempt to maintain objectivity and ensure that all evidence was theory-free would have been presented as the principal difference between the scientific and the religious methods. Yet things are no longer seen as quite that simple. First of all, it is increasingly recognised that objectivity in science is far from easy. The way in which data is collected and the criteria by which it is analysed and presented are both bound up with existing theories. On the other hand, the personal view of a particular scientist should not influence the acceptance or rejection of evidence, or of a theory arising from it. Equally, the overthrow of a previously influential theory is not regarded as a failure, but as a success – since it means that a new theory can emerge that takes even more evidence into account.

By contrast, religion is concerned with personal views, and religion offers a framework of beliefs with which to interpret experience. But that does not prevent religions from making claims about the nature of the universe. Indeed, if a religion makes no factual claims, it is regarded as simply one way of looking at things, with no reason to prefer it over any other – and that will hardly satisfy religious believers. But once factual claims are made, they may be assessed from perspectives other than those of that particular religion.

Example:
We shall look at miracles in chapter 9, but consider what religion means by miracle in the light of this discussion of objectivity. If the account of a 'miracle' makes factual claims of an unusual sort, these can be checked by criteria other than those of the religion itself (in other words, there can be an attempt at objectivity). On the other hand, if by 'miracle' is meant no more than a particular way of viewing an event, there is no reason to challenge its validity, for no factual claims are being made. A traditional 'miracle' tends to claim high factual content, with correspondingly low probability. Something with low factual content and high probability (e.g. that the sun will rise tomorrow) is hardly going to be regarded as a miracle.

---

4 Models and paradigms

Scientific **models** are analogies drawn between something familiar and the object of scientific investigation, in order to help people visualise or understand conceptually what is being studied. These models may need to be revised as the scientific view changes and the analogy no longer holds. For example, until the 19th century, the atom was thought of as a small ball of matter, solid and indivisible. In the early 20th century, that model was no longer adequate, and was replaced by the model that saw the atom as a miniature solar system, with electrons circling round a nucleus like planets round a star.

In the same way, at any one time, the results of scientific work in the past are used as a basis for present research. That is quite inevitable, for otherwise everyone would have to start from scratch every time. These examples of past work, along with their methodologies and concepts, are termed **paradigms**. A paradigm is a general way of looking at a situation, and it tends to survive minor changes in the models that surround it.

Every now and then, however, science makes a radical leap forward, in what may be termed a **paradigm shift**. When that happens, data is re-evaluated in the light of the new paradigm. Otherwise, most scientific work is a routine matter of filling in information within an already existing paradigm. The theory of paradigms was developed by S Kuhn in his influential book *The Structure of Scientific Revolutions* 2nd ed, 1970.

5 The issue of language

At the beginning of the 20th century some philosophers, impressed with the obvious success of the scientific method, sought to analyse language and to show where its meaning could be verified with reference to the sort of evidence that would be appropriate for science. To know if a statement is correct, it is only necessary to check it against the empirical facts upon which it is based. Thus the early work of Wittgenstein, Schlick and others in the Vienna Circle, later to be popularised by A J Ayer in *Language, Truth and Logic*, argued for what is generally known as 'logical positivism', namely that the meaning of a statement is its method of verification. Hence, if I were to say 'There is a cat under the table' it means 'If you look under the table you will see a cat'.

In his book *Tractatus Logico Philosophicus*, Wittgenstein took the view that the function of language was one of picturing the world and thus started with the bold statement:

> The world is everything that is the case.
>
> *(Tractatus 1)*

and equates what can be said with what science can show:

> The totality of true propositions is the whole of natural science.
>
> *(Tractatus 4.11)*

It ends however with the admission that when it comes to the mystical (the intuitive sense of the world as a whole) language fails; we must remain silent. What is 'seen' in a moment of mystical awareness cannot be 'pictured'. It cannot be expressed literally. He ends with:

> Whereof we cannot speak, thereof we must remain silent.

Any statement for which there was no empirical evidence that counted for or against its truth was deemed by the Logical Positivists to be either a tautology, or meaningless. On this basis, logical positivism considered that most religious language was meaningless.

From the middle of the 20th century, however, this view generally gave way to a broader one in which it was recognised that different forms of language functioned in different ways. For example, if I should shout 'Stop!', what I am saying is not meaningless, but it is not a description of anything. I am simply using language to bring something about. Following the later work of Wittgenstein and others, it came to be recognised that different forms of language each have their part to play, and their meaning is given in terms of the form of life within which they operate. Hence religious language was no longer branded as meaningless simply because it did not conform to a norm set by science.

Religious language is misused if it pretends to be scientific. For example, the 'God of the gaps' problem (see page 76) arose because language about God was being used in place of a scientific explanation to fill the gaps in existing knowledge.

For reflection:

- Science sometimes requires an imaginative leap beyond evidence, in order to frame a new hypothesis.
- What is the place of intuition within the scientific process? Like an eye which sees everything other than itself, intuition may underpin much scientific endeavour without ever itself featuring directly within scientific method.

6 The personal and the impersonal in world-views

> **KEY ISSUE**
>
> - The religious quest for certainty, and the factual implications of religious commitment, are contrasted with the provisional nature of scientific claims.

We have seen that making a scientific statement involves an element of risk; if it has any positive content or value there will always be a chance that it will be proved false. But human beings, faced with a world full of risks, may long for certainty. The personal world-views of many religions have appeared to offer that, in contrast with the detached and impersonal weighing of evidence that has characterised the scientific ideal.

a) Certainty and proof

We have seen that, from a scientific point of view, proof is obtained by the best available interpretation of evidence. A hypothesis is put forward and tested out. The proof that something is the case is thus never fixed in an absolute sense – it is a proof based on our present knowledge, always open to the possibility of future revision. Nevertheless, to say that something has been proved to be the case implies that there is adequate evidence to convince a rational person of the truth of a statement. If there is scientific proof for something it would require new evidence, or a clear indication of a misinterpretation of the existing evidence, for that proof to fail.

Therefore, from a scientific point of view, proofs are offered, but there is no absolute certainty that they will continue as proofs. Revision is a possibility. In this sense, a scientist is likely to say 'I am convinced by the evidence that 'X' is the case.' If he or she were to say 'I am absolutely certain that 'X' is the case', that would go beyond what science can claim.

On this basis, it is clear that religion does not really offer absolute proof. Arguments for the existence of God, for example, are open to a variety of interpretations. It is always possible that they will need to be revised. But in the case of religion, a believer may feel 'absolutely certain' of, for example, the existence of God. This certainty is not merely an interpretation of facts, but is born of personal conviction. To be certain of something, implies that you place your trust in it, that you are committed to it. It is to be relied upon, and not open to doubt.

It is possible to be certain of something for which there is no proof. You can say, for example, that you are certain a particular person will arrive on time. You do this on the basis of previous knowledge of that person's behaviour, or his or her general reliability. But clearly there is no way that you can offer proof, that he or she will turn up on this particular occasion.

Of course, previous experience is also the basis of scientific proof. The more consistent are the observations of a particular event, the more likely it will happen again in the future. In this sense, your certainty about a person's behaviour is built up in the same way that a scientific hypothesis is built up. On the other hand, once you say that you feel certain, you have taken a step beyond issues of evidence and the balance of probability; you are committed.

In the Prayer Book service for the burial of the dead, the clergyman speaks of the 'sure and certain hope of the resurrection from the dead'. This does not imply proof of the resurrection, simply an unfailing commitment to belief.

b) An existential approach

Kierkegaard was concerned to show that faith was not a matter of logical conclusions, but of making a personal commitment. It was the intensity of one's personal choice that defined faith. This reflected the earlier Lutheran position, and has characterised much Protestant Christianity. It places personal commitment at the centre of faith, and thus as directly opposed to the process of rational evaluation which characterises the scientific method.

Feelings and attitudes, although described as 'subjective' are a vital part of our experience, if that experience is to be something to which we can relate. Thus, William James (in *The Varieties of Religious Experience*) said:

> To describe the world with all the various feelings of the individual pinch of destiny, all the various spiritual attitudes, left out of the description... would be something like offering a printed bill of fare as the equivalent of a solid meal.

We also saw (above, page 23) how the distinction between primary and secondary qualities seemed to deprive the world of Newtonian physics of all those things that made it rich and beautiful. We have also seen (in Dawkins' *Unweaving the Rainbow*) that there can be a sense of beauty, wonder and poetry in the scientific view of the world.

It is therefore important to distinguish carefully between commitment and emotion or wonder. You can have the latter without the former. You can have a view that includes emotions and aesthetic appreciation, without clinging on to a particular interpretation of that experience. By contrast, commitment is – by definition – something not easily shaken. It implies a determination to maintain a particular view, even in the face of evidence to the contrary.

Example:
The clearest example of religious commitment to a view concerns the problem of evil. Suffering and evil are evidence against the hypothesis that there is an all-loving and all-powerful God. But the religious believer does not see this as a reason to abandon his or her belief, but tries to re-interpret the evidence, find some alternative explanation for it that gives an overall good outcome. In other words, once committed to belief in the existence of God, evidence is either made to fit, ignored, or the whole matter regarded as a mystery. It is precisely this sort of commitment that goes against the methods used by science.

---

7 Authority

> **KEY ISSUE**
>
> ● Authority and acceptance of new ideas plays a part in both scientific and religious communities, with religion divided on its assessment of the value of human reasoning

a) Reason and revelation

Some theologians – especially Thomas Aquinas – have argued that faith is based on both reason and revelation. Through Natural Law, something of God's nature can be known through reason, but that knowledge is supplemented by divine revelation.

By contrast, Luther and other Reformation theologians argued that humankind's reason was subject to the 'Fall' and was therefore incapable of knowing God. If everything that the unaided reason can achieve is futile, faith must be based on revelation and commitment and, if not contrary to reason, at least independent of it.

b) Experience and community

A religious experience has authority for the person who has it. It may give him or her a new perspective on life which colours, or is used to interpret, all that happens. Similarly, a religious organisation, in framing doctrines and moral principles, exerts an authority over its individual members – stemming from the respect that the individual has for the whole body of experience and insight upon which that religion is founded. Religious beliefs therefore depend on authority and are not adopted or changed simply on the basis of reason.

By contrast, scientific enquiry seems to accept no authority other than the commitment to deal rationally with evidence that is presented in an experiment. When we look at the history of science, however, we see that authority plays a part, and that theories only become established once accepted by the scientific community as a whole.

If a scientist comes to a conclusion that is at odds with the views of a majority of his or her colleagues, it may be very difficult to get the results of that scientific work accepted. For example, scientific journals may be unwilling to publish it. From time to time there is a paradigm shift, when the scientific community accepts a very different way of looking at a phenomenon. Before that happens, however, there will be scientists who appear to have to go against accepted scientific principles in order to get the new views established. Thus, science moves forward as theories become widely accepted by the scientific community.

A similar process takes place within religion. Views about the nature of miracles, for example, may gradually come to change. Thus, at the time when Hume was writing, he probably reflected the view of a majority of religious people when he referred to a miracle as a violation of a law of nature. Today, a majority of religious people would not want to take that point of view, or would qualify it considerably (see below, page 95).

It is therefore inaccurate to suggest that science is based on reason while religion is based on authority: both make claims that depend to some extent on both reason and authority. The essential difference, however, is that the scientific method accepts that every claim may be challenged in the light of new evidence.

A Buddhist view

In this book we are concerned primarily with theism and the Western religions. Notice however that Buddhism is far closer to modern science, both in terms of its view of life, and also its methodology:

> At the heart of Buddhism and in particular at the heart of the Great Vehicle (the Mahayana), great importance is placed on analytical reasoning. This view holds that we should not accept any teaching of the Buddha's if we were to find any flaw or inconsistency in the reasoning of that teaching. It is advisable, therefore, to adopt a sceptical attitude and retain a critical mind, even with regard to the Buddha's own words. Does he himself not say ... 'O Bhikshu, as gold is tested by rubbing, cutting, and melting, accept my word only on analysis and not simply out of respect.'
>
> Dalai Lama *Beyond Dogma*, p181

Summary List

- Deduction and induction: methodology used by science
- The attempt to achieve objectivity
- Science progresses via the establishing and eventual replacement of paradigms
- Logical Positivists and others attempted to limit meaningful language to what could be evidenced
- The religious quest for certainty does not square with the provisional nature of scientific statements
- Authority plays a part in both religious and scientific communities.

Essay Questions

1a Discuss the view that science looks for proof, while religion looks for certainty.

OR

1b For religion, unlike science, certainty is possible but proof is impossible. Discuss.

2. To what extent can it be argued that religion and science rely on completely different sources of knowledge?

(For a question like this, one might start with a traditional distinction between scientific evidence and religious revelation, then move on to show how evidence comes value-laden, and perhaps how religion adapts to the prevailing scientific view.)

3.

Science seems to me to teach in the highest and strongest manner the great truth which is embodied in the Christian conception of entire surrender to the will of God: sit down before fact as a little child, be prepared to give up every preconceived notion, follow humbly and to whatever abysses nature leads, or you shall learn nothing.

(letter from T. H. Huxley to Charles Kingsley, 23rd September 1860)

Can a Christian ever follow Huxley's advice and set aside all preconceived notions, including religious convictions, when examining evidence? Illustrate your answer with reference to the methods used to gain and evaluate scientific and religious truth.

(Ask yourself: Do most people adopt a religious faith after carefully weighing the evidence for its truth? If 'yes' – which features of the modern scientific world view should they take into account? If 'no' – what other reasons are there for adopting a faith? Do they depend upon any particular view of the world?)

7 The Origin of the Universe

1 Dimensions

Cosmology – the study of the nature of the universe as a whole – goes beyond the search for a mathematical theory to explain its origin and development. It seldom remains simply a quest for information, for it raises questions about the meaning and value of human life. Theories about the universe (whether they are ancient, medieval or modern) carry with them implications for understanding how the human enterprise fits into their overall schemes, and whether it can have any lasting significance. Quite apart from any religious theories of creation, this fact alone places cosmology at the heart of issues connecting religion and science.

The 20th century saw a dramatic change in the understanding of the dimensions and age of the universe. In this, as in many areas of science, details are always being revised, so the figures here should be taken only as a general guide. The universe is estimated to consist of at least ten billion galaxies, each composed of stars and gas clouds. Our own galaxy (the central area of which is represented by the stars of the Milky Way) is spiral in shape and rotates. It is thought to contain 100 billion stars, and to be about 100,000 light years in diameter. (A light year is the distance travelled by light in a year, at a speed of 186,000 miles per second.) The Sun is a smallish star, about 32,000 light years from the centre of the galaxy.

Looking out into space is also looking back in time. If I observe a galaxy ten million light years away, I observe it as it was ten million years ago (when the light from it started its journey towards me) not as it is now. Imagine observers placed at different points in the universe, all looking at the Earth. They would see – unfolding in their present – events which are in our past. From nearby stars in our own galaxy, they see the building of mediaeval cathedrals or Egyptian pyramids. From stars at the far side of our galaxy, they see only primitive man. From the nearest galaxy cluster to ours (8 million light years away), it is too early for an observer to see even man-like apes, and from galaxies more than 5 billion light years away (less than half way across the known universe) there is nothing to be seen here but clouds of cosmic dust, for our sun and its planets have not yet been formed.

And what of life itself, as we imagine observing it from these distances? It is but a chance and fleeting film of blue and green upon a tiny planet, lost in a galaxy of a hundred thousand million stars, itself lost within a universe of ten thousand million galaxies. And all this matter is but an exception to the rule of emptiness; grains of sand spread thinly through a void.

Some theories about the nature of the universe are equally thought provoking. Einstein suggested that the universe could be seen as a **hypersphere**. If you start at a point on the surface of a sphere and move off in any direction, you never come to an edge, although the actual surface of the sphere is finite. In the same way, Einstein suggested that you could move through a finite universe without reaching an edge, eventually returning to your staring point.

Events and the past

In December 1997, astronomers witnessed the biggest explosion since the 'big bang' (see below), a blast of high-energy gamma radiation, lasting for one second and releasing as much energy as the 10 billion, trillion stars in the known universe. Yet it took place in a region only about 100 miles across. The light from the explosion took about 12 billion years to reach Earth. In other words, it took place 8 billion years before Earth was formed. How do you find a religious concept of creation that copes with events and dimensions such as this?

---

a) The Big Bang theory

Evidence for the past state of the universe is made possible by observing trends in the present and projecting them back into the past. At this moment, it can be observed that the galaxies are flying apart. Those furthest away from us are moving away faster than those nearer to us. From this we infer that at one time all the galaxies were closer together, and that they are moving apart in all directions.

On this basis, we can tell how far away a galaxy is by how fast it is moving away from us. The spectrum of light changes if the body being observed is moving away at very great speed. In 1929 E. P. Hubble observed a 'red shift' in the light coming from distant galaxies, which led to the theory that the universe is expanding in all directions. From the speed of expansion, it is possible to calculate the age of the universe.

It is generally believed that the universe started with a 'hot big bang' somewhere between 10 and 20 billion years ago. The point from which the present universe expanded out in an explosion of enormous energy and heat is termed a **spacetime singularity**. It is a point **from which** space and time have come, not a point **within** space and time. This is an essential feature of the theory. In an ordinary explosion, matter is flung outwards through space. In the 'big bang', what we know as space and time are created simultaneously with that event. It is as though we are in an expanding bubble.

The theory predicts that at one time all the matter in the universe was spread out uniformly as a hot gas. This gradually cooled and condensed to form stars and galaxies. In the 1960s background microwave radiation at 3 degrees above absolute zero was found throughout the universe, and this is thought to be the remnant of the heat from that early phase. The theory also predicted the existence throughout the universe of stable, light elements (including, principally, hydrogen) produced at the earliest stage (unlike heavier elements, which were formed later in stars), and this has been found to be the case.

An alternative theory (the Steady State Theory) was proposed in the 1950s by Hoyle, Bondi and Gold. They argued that as the universe expands, new matter is created so that its density remains constant. A series of 'mini big bangs' producing galaxies ensued. This has largely given way to a broad acceptance of the standard big bang theory.

Modern cosmology is a fascinating and ever-developing branch of study. The big bang may have been triggered by what is called an 'instanton', a point of fleeting existence, outside time and space, which immediately triggers an infinite, expanding, open universe. For our purposes, however, such details do not matter. The fact is that science has established a generally accepted theory for the origin and structure of the universe, a theory which is compatible with the best available evidence.

b) World without end?

Following the Second Law of Thermodynamics, the universe should gradually dissipate its energy and end up in a state of total entropy (uniform disorder) and heat death. On the other hand, it is possible that, as the universe continues to expand, it will reach a point at which the energy of expansion is reduced to a point at which it is balanced by the gravitational pull, and at that point the universe would start to contract, eventually imploding into a 'big crunch'. Possibly also, as a result of the violent compression of the universe into this singularity, there could be another 'big bang' with a new universe being formed.

Whatever the fate of the universe, the Earth has a limited life, for as the Sun uses up its fuel it will change into a 'red giant', incinerating and absorbing the Earth as it does so. Even this is a distant prospect, for, at about 5000 million years of age, the Sun is only about half way through its present life.

As with considerations about the origin of the universe, one needs to ask whether such views about the end of the world as we know it can have any significance for religion. The scale within which the Christian imagery of the world ending and Christ returning to judge people is totally different from predictions about universal heat death. It originates from a time when the Earth was seen as the centre of the universe. The only really significant issue here is whether language about the end of the world need to be taken literally, or whether it is a way of expressing those values that the religion holds to be 'final', in the sense of ultimate.

c) The limits of what can be known

It is important to recognise that the nature and dimensions of the universe are determined by the faculties by which we perceive it. There is a theoretical limit to what can be known. It is not merely that, one day, we will develop a telescope that will get us 'beyond' the known universe, it is that the universe and our experience of it are bound up together – they are one and the same thing.

We cannot get 'outside' the universe. The **deist** idea of an external creator and designer is simply illogical, in that an external 'god' would be entirely unknowable.

2 Creatio ex nihilo

The Christian doctrine of creation is that God created the world out of nothing (*creatio ex nihilo*) rather than out of any pre-existing material. This was important in the 4th century, to distinguish orthodox Christianity from the 'gnostic' view that matter was evil – since it could not have been evil if dirctly created by God.

To appreciate its later significance, consider the **deist** view of God as an external agent and designer. For the deist, God and the world are two separate things, in that God is located 'outside' the world. In a sense, His being there or not makes no difference to the workings of the world – it is like a machine that he has created and left to run on its own. The theist view, by contrast, is of a God who is both immanent within and yet transcends the world. Whatever is happening in the world is therefore seen as part of God's activity – there is no separate material order with which he is not concerned.

In quantum theory, sub-atomic particles come into existence without having a particular antecedent cause, and a quantum understanding of gravity might therefore conceive of spacetime being created out of nothing with the same unpredictability. Quantum theory therefore appears to be more compatible with the idea of *creatio ex nihilo* than the older Newtonian physics. These ideas are discussed by Paul Davies in his book *God and the New Physics*.

However, saying that a particle can appear from nowhere is not really relevant to the idea of God creating the universe out of nothing. The crucial thing to appreciate is that the Christian doctrine of creation is about **agency** (that God made the world) whereas the 'big bang' and other theories are about the **mechanisms** by which the world came into existence. A theist could quite well say that the 'big bang' was the mechanism by which the world came about, whilst still holding that God was the agent of that creation.

3 God: 'Being Itself' or external agent?

KEY ISSUE

● What kind of 'god' is compatible with the dimensions of the universe?

There are a number of different ways in which religious thinkers approach the idea of creation. At one extreme there is creationism, which was a religious response to the issue of human origins and evolution, both in the 19th century and up to the present day (see above page 37). But Creationists generally refuse to accept any of the modern theories about the origins of the universe, since they believe that the universe was created only a few thousand years ago, as described in the Bible. Sometimes they seek to give alternative explanations for the scientific findings. Thus, for example, the Australian creationist Barry Setterfield has argued that the speed of light has diminished since creation, which accounts for the 'red shift' phenomenon, and that the universe is therefore much younger than was thought.

Even when they present alternative hypotheses which appear to be scientific, or which are based on scientific evidence, it is clear that creationists are not seeking an answer with an open mind. Their aim is to prove the case for what they hold to be true on religious grounds.

By contrast, John Macquarrie (in his *Principles of Christian Theology*) takes an existential approach to the doctrine of creation, by examining what it says about human meaning and values. He argues that, if you believe yourself to be a creature made by God, you will be answerable to him, subject to his demands and feel yourself to be a recipient of his grace. The opposite view (which would be taken by someone who did not see God as the agent of creation) would be one in which you feel yourself to be independent, self-directing, and not answerable to anything outside yourself.

Clearly, by turning the issue of creation into an existential one, he separates its religious importance from any scientific view about the origins of the universe. The existential approach makes factual claims about God and creation irrelevant – what matters is the personal significance of that belief.

As we have seen, **deism** is the view that God is an external creator and designer. The actual mechanism by which the world unfolds is irrelevant to such a belief, all that is required is the sense that the world displays some form of intelligent design.

Equally, a **pantheist** has few problems with views about the origin of the world, since this belief simply identifies God and the world – theories about the world are theories about God, simply that.

For the **theist** and **panentheist** however, the matter is not quite that simple. Both views present God as immanent within and yet transcending the physical world (and the latter is really only an extension of the former, emphasising the immanence of God). The problem here is that God is seen as engaged and active within the world, taking a continuing creative role. How does that role (or that agency) square with scientific explanations? One of the problems here concerns the temptation to 'locate' God's activity in gaps in the scientific explanation of things.

a) God of the gaps

As science explains something, there seems no need to suggest that it was brought about by God. The more science explains, the smaller become the gaps into which God's activity can be fitted. The classic example of this was the reply given by the mathematician Pierre Laplace (1749-1827) who, when asked where God came into his astronomical calculations, declared 'I have no need of that hypothesis.'

Thus, for example, Aquinas needed an 'unmoved mover' to explain present movement. With Newton, however, all movement follows fixed laws, and objects continue either at rest or in uniform motion in a straight line unless acted upon by external forces. Present movement is therefore entirely predictable. At most, all that is required is some initial force to start the whole thing going. God is therefore located right outside such a mechanical universe.

As the explanation of cosmic origins improves, or medical knowledge explains an unexpected recovery from disease, so the 'gaps' into which God can be fitted diminish. The problem was put very succinctly by J Habgood:

> In a world made up of objects, God has to be thought of either as an object or as a concept. If the former, there seems to be less and less space for him in our scheme of things as scientific knowledge advances; if the latter, religion is a private fantasy.

Religion and Science, p141

The theologian Paul Tillich argued that God should be described as 'Being Itself' rather than 'a being', and this is relevant to the 'gaps' dilemma. If God is thought of as a being among others, there becomes less and less room for him. But the very idea of God being an object within the world could, from a theistic point of view, be regarded as idolatry. The whole essence of classical theism is that God is both **immanent** (within the world) and **transcendent** (beyond the world). Such a balance does not allow God to be identified with any one thing. Hence, the quest for a 'gap' for God is mistaken. As 'Being Itself', 'God' is a term to be used for the whole of reality, not part of it.

4 The Anthropic Principle

> **KEY ISSUE**
> • Does the structure of the universe make it inevitable that human life should appear and, if so, what conclusions might be drawn from this?

There are certain fundamental features of the universe that have enabled it to develop in the particular way it has. If the universe had developed differently, we would not be here: that much is clear. What conclusions should we draw from that fact? One answer to this question is known as 'the anthropic principle'.

> Imagine a universe in which one or another of the fundamental constants of physics is altered by a few percent one way or the other. Man could never come into being in such a universe. That is the central point of the anthropic principle. According to this principle, a life-giving factor lies at the centre of the whole machinery and design of the world.

The Anthropic Cosmological Principle Barrow and Tipler, Oxford, 1986

There are weak and strong versions of the anthropic principle:

• **weak:** if the major constants of the universe were different, we would not be here, life would not have evolved

- **strong**: the universe contains within itself the potential for life, such that it was impossible for human life not to have appeared.

The weak version causes no problems, it merely states the obvious. But the strong form seems to imply that the whole development of the universe took place in the way that it did **so that** human life should appear.

Stephen Hawking comments:

> [The strong anthropic principle]... runs against the tide of the whole history of science. We have developed from the geocentric cosmologies of Ptolemy and his forebears, through the heliocentric cosmology of Copernicus and Galileo, to the modern picture in which the earth is a medium-sized planet orbiting around an average star in the outer suburbs of an ordinary spiral galaxy, which is itself only one of about a million million galaxies in the observable universe. Yet the strong anthropic principle would claim that this whole vast construction exists simply for our sake. This is very hard to believe. Our Solar System is certainly a prerequisite for our existence, and one might extend this to the whole of our galaxy to allow for an earlier generation of stars that created the heavier elements. But there does not seem to be any need for all those other galaxies, nor for the universe to be so uniform and similar in every direction on the large scale.'

A Brief History of Time, p126

The logic behind the anthropic principle would seem to run like this:

- if the universe were different, we would not be here
- everything in the universe is determined causally, once the initial parameters are set
- therefore, given the parameters, life had to evolve.

Nothing is wrong with that, but the implication is then made that the initial parameters **had** to be what they are. Here we come against the problem of chance and necessity. Consider the chance of two people meeting in the street:

- everything I have ever been, and everything that has happened in the world, has contributed in some way to the fact that I am in this place at this time
- the same thing applies to you
- therefore the odds **against us** meeting up by chance are almost infinite, since they depend upon an almost infinite number of prior events.

But, given that every event has a cause, then, given the way the world is, it is **inevitable** that we should meet. **Thus, in a world in which everything interconnects, every event is both highly unlikely but (with hindsight) also inevitable.**

The problem with the strong version of the anthropic principle may be illustrated by the use of the word 'must'. Consider the two statements:

1 'Fancy seeing you here this early, you **must** have got the 6.30 train!'
2 'You **must** get the 6.30 train!'

Whilst the second is a command, the first is merely a deduction. The strong version of the anthropic principle starts with a deduction, and then makes it appear to be a command.

Extreme care therefore needs to be taken by anyone who thinks that the anthropic principle can be taken as evidence for a designer god, or as in some way placing humankind in a privileged position within the universe. The logic or the weak form of the argument does not warrant either conclusion, and although the strong version could support them, its logic is flawed.

Summary List

● What are the religious implications of the view of the universe revealed by modern cosmology?
● Theism does not accept the idea of pre-existing matter, separate from its creator
● The 'god of the gaps' problem helps shift religious focus from an external 'deist' view of God to one that involves both transcendence and immanence
● The Anthropic Principle is problematic for supporting religious claims of divine providence.

Essay Questions

1. Explain what is meant by 'the god of the gaps', and how this problem has come about. Suggest how a religious person might present a concept of God that did not require a 'gap'.
(Clearly, a question such as this is looking for a religious evaluation of the adequacy of different ideas of 'God'. It also gives scope for a consideration of miracles or freedom, as possible 'gaps' that people have sought for 'God'.)

2. How far has modern science shown that the universe does not need a creator?

3. The Anthropic Principle is a modern version of the argument from design. Discuss.

8 Freedom and Determinism

1 An historical perspective

The first thinker to have tackled the issue of determinism was Democritus, a Greek philosopher of the 5th century BCE. He was one of the '**atomists**', who developed the idea – remarkable for that time, although commonplace to us – that everything consisted of atoms in space. He argued that objects existed independent of our observation of them, and that it was possible, in theory, to predict how each and every thing would behave.

He also came to the conclusion that atoms could not have emerged out of nothing, and that they were therefore eternal. However, individual atoms grouped together to form complex entities (all the objects of our visible world) which were constantly changing as their component atoms dispersed to form other things. In other words, you have an eternal, material world, in which all the things that we experience are composite and temporary collections of atoms.

This view of the universe (which was taken up by the Epicureans) created a problem in terms of human freedom and the purpose of life, for it saw the whole universe as a single determined mechanism, operating on impersonal laws. Since we are temporary, composite creatures, we might as well make the most of such pleasure as can be had in this life, knowing that it will inevitably come to an end.

The problem of freedom and determinism was given religious impetus by St Augustine, in connection with the nature of evil. He presented what was to become the traditional dilemma that, if God is omnipotent (all powerful) and omniscient (all knowing), he both knows and is able to control all that we do. How then can we be held responsible for any evil we do?

Augustine saw evil as a sign of the fallen nature of humankind, but because God gives people free will, they are responsible for whatever they do. On the other hand, in order to maintain the omniscience of God, he argued for predestination: that God knows already who is to be saved and who damned, and that we can do nothing to alter that judgement.

Clearly, such views do not square easily with the notions of freedom, morality, conscience or justice. **Why should I be damned by God for something which God has already determined will happen?**

With the rise of science, the mechanistic view of the universe given by Newtonian physics suggested that everything in the world may be described in terms of laws which operate with mathematical precision. If all the laws of nature were known, it would be possible to predict exactly what would happen in each and every situation in the future, given a complete knowledge of the world as it is now. Everything is determined. Following the same scientific principles, any event that is unexpected is not generally ascribed to divine intervention, but is thought to have been caused by the operation of factors and laws that are not yet understood. Thus science assumes that everything has a cause – or indeed a large number of causes working together – which determine exactly what it is and how it has come about. One of the most definite statements of this was made by Pierre Laplace (1749–1827):

> An intelligence knowing at any instant of time, all forces acting in nature, as well as the momentary positions of all things of which the universe consists, would be able to comprehend the motion of the largest bodies of the world and those of the smallest atoms in one simple formula, provided it were sufficiently powerful to subject all data to analysis, to it nothing would be uncertain, both future and past would be present before its eyes.
>
> quoted in Paul Davies, *Superforce*, 1984, p38

This view has implications both for human freedom and morality, and also for the idea of divine providence – God intervening in the world, setting aside its laws, for some special purpose.

The religious emphasis on the issue of freedom and determinism therefore moved on to take this mechanistic view into account. We have already seen that Descartes made a radical distinction between the physical and the mental worlds. I am a thinking being linked to a physical body that is part of a predictable, physical universe. His concern was to see how a mental operation (having a particular thought or desire, deciding to do something) could have a physical result. How does my thinking actually make something happen in a physical universe that is controlled by the laws of nature?

Cartesian dualism and the rise of modern science resulted in the perception of a mechanical universe, totally conditioned and determined, every movement theoretically predictable, within which human beings had thoughts and desires, chose what to do and acted in a way that they experienced as being free. What is more, in order to be religious or moral, it seems absolutely necessary to be free to choose how to act. The fear, from a religious point of view, was that a totally conditioned universe would leave no place for either religion or morality.

The key issue here for religion and science is the extent to which science, in the predictions it makes, is able to claim that everything is determined by established laws, principles or statistical expectations. If science can explain everything in terms of its causes, where is there room for freedom and choice?

2 Leibniz – God's chosen world

The philosopher and mathematician Leibniz (1646-1716) saw God as an eternal and infinite mind who saw and determined everything in the created order and who had chosen to make the world exactly as it is. Looking at the world as a whole, Leibniz argued that, because one thing may be incompatible with or dependent upon another, a change in any one individual thing in the world would require that everything else be changed as well. In other words, there may be a number of possible worlds, in which things are quite different from those we find in this one, but within this particular world, everything has to be as it is. In addition, since he believed that it would have been possible for God to have created any sort of world, he argued that – since God chose to create this one – it must be the best possible. Two things follow from this:

1 Within this world we cannot predict exactly what will happen, since we do not have God's infinite mind and therefore cannot see the way everything works together. Therefore, not knowing that we are completely determined, we actually experience ourselves as free. In other words (not those of Leibniz), freedom is not knowing all the reasons why you do what you do.
2 A world within which there is human free will, and in which there can therefore be the evil and suffering that come from its misuse, is to be judged better than a world which lacks freedom but is free from its evils. He argued this on the grounds that a perfect God would create the best of all possible worlds.

But notice here that there is still a great difference between what is experienced (freedom) and what is actually the case (a world totally determined by the mind of God). How can these be related in such a way that the one does not undermine the other? This question was taken up again by Kant.

3 Kant – determined but free

KEY ISSUE
● At one and the same time I may appear to be determined, but know myself to be free

One way out of this dilemma was given by **Immanuel Kant (1724–1804)**, in his *Critique of Pure Reason*. He distinguished between:

- phenomena (things as we experience them) and
- noumena (things as they are in themselves).

He considered that the mind can understand phenomena by means of the concepts of space, time and causality. In other words, we do not say that everything has a cause because we have been able to check and identify a cause for each and every event (which would be impossible) but because our minds are so organised that they assume that everything they experience is an effect for which there has been a cause.

Within the world of phenomena, therefore, everything is subject to causation (just as everything is located in time and space) – because that is the only way our minds can understand it. On the other hand, I know that I am free to choose and to act. I experience freedom, although, in the external phenomenal world, I cannot detect it. **Kant therefore saw the individual as phenomenally determined but noumenally free.** Everything I see in the external world is determined, but that is because of the way my mind works and perceives things, but I experience my own freedom – it is one of the presuppositions of every choice I make.

In a sense, the implication of Kant's argument for the religious debate on this is that, rather than seeing some things as conditioned and others as free, it is possible to see everything as both conditioned and free. This has the added advantage of not letting human freedom get into a 'God of the gaps' problem (see page 76) where freedom is found only in the 'gaps' that have not been explained and cannot yet be predicted.

Kant's argument, in seeing the mind as having an active rather than a passive role in terms of understanding the world, marked a major turning point in the history of Western philosophy. It also serves to reinforce a fundamental self/word distinction which raises a whole range of questions about minds and bodies and their interactions. Everything I freely choose to do will be seen as totally determined by an omnipotent external observer.

We should also note that both Leibniz and Kant wrote against the background of the 17th and 18th century approach to science, dominated by Newton. Their struggle is to understand how the Newtonian mechanism squares with the experience of freedom. However, the freedom / determinism issue has moved on from there, mainly because of new ways of approaching the role of religion, and also changes in the perception of science and in the way science has moved far beyond the narrow confines of the Newtonian world.

4 A romantic challenge?

In the 19th century there was a move away from the mechanistic views of the 17th and 18th centuries, and a drive to experience nature in a more feeling, less abstract way. This is part of what is generally termed the 'romantic movement', and it highlights the problems of trying to experience the world in the way in which science had described it.

'The stars,' she whispers, 'blindly run.'

This line, from Tennyson's poem *In Memoriam*, encapsulates the whole dilemma. If everything 'blindly runs', then the human body 'blindly runs', without freedom and without responsibility for its actions.

Of course, one way out of this was to seek a very different basis for religion. The theologian Schleiermacher described religion as 'the sense and taste for the infinite', thus locating it very personally in the way in which human beings responded to life, rather than in the mechanistic world 'out there'. Religion could therefore retreat into being concerned with feelings and tastes, severing itself from the world of science.

Such reactions only served to confirm the gulf in people's minds between the 'objective' world and our 'subjective' experience of it. This can be expressed through various dualistic contrasts:

- Mind and Body
- God and the Universe
- Freedom and Determinism
- Faith and Reason
- Arts and Sciences.

In each of these pairs, the first is based on a personal experience of, and relationship with the world; the second is based on mechanical and physical theories which have been abstracted from experience, and by which experience is then interpreted.

The central dilemma of the freedom and determinism debate rests on the fact that we know we are free, but that as soon as we try to apply our abstracted theories to that freedom, it becomes part of a mechanical and determined system. The fundamental mistake here is in thinking that the mechanistic system, which informs me that I am determined, is somehow more 'real' than my own experience of freedom and choice.

5 Haeckel and Monod – a naturalistic view

> **KEY ISSUE**
>
> - 'Scientific materialism' is the attempt to show that all knowledge and reality is a product of the material world and depends upon its laws. It therefore dismisses morality and religion as the product of superstition, since it cannot be validated scientifically

a) The temptations of scientific determinism

In 1899, Ernst Haeckel published *The Riddle of the Universe*. He argued that everything, including thought, was the product of the material world and was absolutely controlled and determined by its laws. Freedom was an illusion and religion a superstition. He proposed what is generally termed 'scientific materialism', popularising Darwin's theory of evolution, and sweeping away all earlier philosophy which did not fit his naturalistic and scientific outlook.

On the other hand (as we shall see in the chapter on the self – page 108) he did not deny that there was a 'soul' or self, rather he saw these things as natural phenomena, and as based on a material substratum. He was totally opposed to Descartes' dualism, with matter on one side and mind on the other. He is sometimes described as a materialist, but this is not strictly true (since it implies the non-existence of the world of thought, the self, and freedom), what he actually claims is that all the 'spiritual' aspects of humanity arise out of and are dependent upon their material basis – and this he saw as a 'naturalistic' view of the universe.

His was also a 'monist' view: that there is one single reality, not two. Haeckel clearly believed that the doctrines of religion were based on superstition, encouraged by the notion of a dualistic universe in which mind or spirit were separated off from matter. He considered that, with further progress, science would lead to a unified system of thought that would explain absolutely everything.

He claimed of his view that:

> ... it involves, on its positive side, the essential unity of the cosmos and the causal connection of all phenomena that come within its congnizance, but it also, in a negative way, marks the highest intellectual progress, in that it definitely rules out the three central dogmas of metaphysics – God, freedom and immortality. In assigning mechanical causes to phenomena everywhere, the law of substance comes into line with the universal law of causality.

The Riddle of the Universe

It is clear, however, celebrating the end of a century of achievement in the sciences, that he felt that physics in particular had established itself beyond question and was now the dominant force in human understanding. It is interesting to reflect on the fact that the sort of physics he regarded as so soundly established was soon to be challenged by radical leaps forward. What would Haeckel have made of relativity and quantum theory? Would they have changed his views on the nature of determinism?

However much the scientific theories may have changed, the fundamental issue raised by Haeckel remained throughout the 20th century: his form of scientific materialism basically considered science to be the only reliable route to knowledge, and matter to be the fundamental reality.

Jacques Monod explored the implications of molecular biology, and in particular the fact that evolutionary change is brought about by random mutations at the genetic level. He therefore argued that everything that takes place at higher levels of organisation (e.g. for a human being) is ultimately the result of chance. Once the chance mutations have actually take place however, everything else follows from them of necessity. Chance and necessity between them therefore determine all that will happen. This view excludes any possibility of there being a God. In *Chance and Necessity* (1972) he claimed:

> pure chance, absolutely free but blind, is at the very root of the stupendous edifice of evolution.

and concluded by saying:

> ... man at last knows that he is alone in the unfeeling immensity of the universe, out of which he emerged only by chance.

Notice that this view of humankind's place within the universe, which sounds rather bleak and impersonal, has prompted other thinkers to propose the 'anthropic principle' (see page 76) in order to take a more positive and integrated view.

Now let us examine the implications of Haeckel or Monod for the specific issue of freedom and determinism. Although as scientists they inhabited very different worlds, fundamentally they take the same position:

- Everything that happens depends on physical laws. Haeckel thought these could be determined; Monod (in the light of the 20th century advances in biology) sees the determined aspect of such physical laws as based on random, chance mutations.
- Neither of them will accept a dualistic universe where human freedom and thought stands over against a determined physical universe.

Monod was concerned to remove the idea of a creator god, shaping the development of evolution – the whole process was explained by chance and necessity. You do not need God in order to explain how the universe has come to be as it is. But the same argument can be applied to human freedom. To experience freedom and choice is to be creative – in a limited sense, it is to be god-like (and religion therefore makes much of the idea of freedom being given to humankind by God). Whatever I think I have freely chosen to do, will (to follow the line of Monod's argument) be explicable in terms of chance (the particular circumstances and opportunities that were presented) and necessity (the laws of nature that, with hindsight, we can see as determining the choice that is made).

Between them, according to Monod, chance and necessity have provided an exhaustive account of what is experienced as free choice.

6 A quantum view

A characteristic feature of quantum physics is Heisenberg's **uncertainly principle**. This states that it is possible to know either the position or the momentum of any particle, but not to know both accurately at the same time. In dealing with particles, it also appears that their behaviour is random – they are not 'caused', as are events on a larger scale. Hence, as we saw above (page 57), quantum physics deals with probability rather than with individual certainty at the sub-atomic level.

It is sometimes argued that this 'uncertainty principle' has revealed an element of chance or freedom at the heart of reality, and that this somehow allows for freedom rather than determinism at the level of human activity. But this is not justified. In quantum physics, simple events are undetermined – we cannot know what any one particle is going to do. What we do know, however, is what very large numbers of particles are likely to do. The quantum approach is therefore statistical.

Take a parallel example: voting in elections. After various exit polls have been taken, political commentators predict with increasing accuracy what the final result of an election will be. Indeed, most of the interest at election time focuses on those constituencies that are marginal. On the other hand, it is impossible for anyone to know which way any one individual person will vote when he or she enters the polling booth.

Two things follow from this:

1 nature can still be regular and predictable, even if at the sub-atomic level individual particles are undetermined
2 therefore, at the level at which human freedom operates (or appears to operate), quantum indeterminacy is irrelevant. On the large scale, it is as unlikely that statistical probability will be overturned as that a 'law of nature' will be broken.

Indeed Erwin Schrödinger concluded his discussion of this issue by saying:

Quantum physics has nothing to do with the free-will problem.

Science and Humanism, p67

7 Playing dice?

Einstein commented on the idea of indeterminacy by saying 'God does not play dice.' By this he meant that is it impossible to conceive of a universe in which everything happens in a random fashion. The whole of our ability to think and predict is based on the perception of regularity. Indeed, the whole success of the scientific endeavour is proof of the consistency of the phenomenal world. If things behaved in random fashion, no science or technology would be possible, for it works by predicting and examining the results of predictions.

From the religious perspective it is also important to realise that two extremes are equally difficult to square with religion and morality: the absolute determinism of a mechanical universe, and the absolute freedom of a universe that operates in a totally random fashion. Randomness precludes any sense of meaning, purpose or value.

There are two ways of examining any complex situation: by taking a reductionist approach or a holistic one. From a **reductionist** point of view, reality is found in the smallest component parts of any complex entity (e.g. you are 'nothing but' the molecules, atoms and sub-atomic particles of which you are comprised). If it can be shown that your constituent particles behave in a random fashion, then you, as a whole, are considered to be random, lacking any overall purpose. From a **holistic** point of view, reality is seen in the complex entity itself, rather than in its parts (e.g. there is something that is 'you' over and above the existence of all the separate molecules that make you up).

Generally speaking, reductionist approaches deny freedom, either by showing sub-atomic randomness (and therefore the lack of purposeful choice that freedom implies), or by denying any freedom of action by reducing everything to the mechanical rules that determine the operation of each component. Holistic approaches, by contrast, see freedom as a feature of complex systems.

The act of thinking and perceiving is one that involves a holistic approach. My eyes may scan and see a nose, a pair of eyes, hair, chin, clothes and so on. But my mind immediately puts those sensations together, checks them against memory, and experiences them together as comprising a particular person I know. Random perception would make nonsense of all human thought. Hence the importance of Einstein's point: that ultimately you cannot think and encounter the world on the basis of randomness. For any science to make sense (as well as religion) there has to be the presupposition that the world itself makes sense, and for that there has to be some form of holistic view.

For reflection:
In this chapter we have looked briefly at some of the main areas of philosophical and scientific thinking that shape our ideas of freedom and determinism. What is clear is that **freedom is a phenomenon of the present, determinism of the past**. In other words, once a free choice has been made, it can be examined from the point of view of its circumstances and the motives that lie behind it. That process leads to the view that the choice was quite inevitable – and thus determined. **Looking back, we see reasons, and the world looks fixed; looking forward, we see choices, and the world looks free. In the present we experience a limited ability to make a difference; our world is plastic.**

Summary List

- Materialism and determinism has a long history, going back to the atomists of ancient Greece
- Leibniz argued that, since everything was interconnected, nothing could change without having universal consequence
- Kant argued that causality was the product of the way our minds work, and therefore that everything we experience is determined by it. On the other hand we experience ourselves as free
- Scientific materialism dismisses all religion and morality; everything requires a material basis
- Quantum uncertainty is not relevant to issues of human freedom
- A reductionist view leads to determinism; an holistic view is able to show freedom

Essay Questions

1. Is it possible for you to perceive my freedom?
   (This might best be approached by looking at Kant's distinction between phenomena and noumena. It is essentially about how to square the experience of freedom with the determinist tendencies inherent in perception and the scientific approach to explanation and causality.)

2. Leibniz argued that this must be the best possible world. If so, can you change any part of it without making it, on the whole, worse? Discuss.
   (This question invites a consideration of the interconnected nature of all phenomena, but also the sense that personal freedom implies the ability to choose and thus change the world. It also raises the question of value in a materially determined universe – an issue relevant to Haeckel, Monod and the Logical Positivist movement in the early 20th century, for which see page 64.)

9 Miracles

KEYWORDS

prescriptive and descriptive – a law is descriptive if it simply describes what happens; it becomes prescriptive if it indicates what should happen

1 Historical background

In the biblical world, events were not thought of as determined by fixed laws of nature, but open to spiritual influence. God was believed to uphold the natural order, and his will was seen especially in unusual events – signs and wonders, healings and exorcisms. The question asked was not 'How did that happen?' but 'What does it mean?' or 'Why did God choose to act in this way?'. However crudely the images of God may be presented (e.g. as someone who goes into battle, or stops the movement of the sun, to help his chosen people), the biblical view is certainly theism rather than deism – in other words, God is thought of as active within the world, not simply a detached, external creator, uninvolved with his creation.

The same view of an active and purposeful God is reflected in broadly based religious attitudes today. If a person asks 'Why should this happen to me?' when suddenly struck down by an illness, he or she is not really looking for an answer in terms of infections and immune systems. Rather, the quest is for some explanation which enables that person to make sense of the illness in the context of his or her life as a whole. For the believer in God, that amounts to asking why God has chosen that this should happen. Miracles were all part of this world-view – a world in which certain events are interpreted as the result of God's direct action.

With the mechanistic explanation of the universe offered by Newtonian physics, the perception of miracles changed; they were seen as violations of the laws of nature. But since God was seen as the designer who had established the world on regular mathematical principles, miracles was seen by some as an unnecessary continuation of beliefs from a former unenlightened age of superstition rather than science. Thus, for example Toland's book *Christianity not Mysterious* (1696) argues that Christianity should be stripped of its irrational elements, including its miracles.

Not all who saw God as a designer wanted to be rid of the miraculous. Newton himself accepted that God might intervene in the world, and William Paley (who re-formulated the design argument for the existence of God) saw miracles as proof of Christ's divinity (in his *Evidences of Christianity*, 1794).

We therefore need to consider three issues:

1 Can there ever be sufficient evidence to prove that a miracle (if this means a violation of a law of nature) has taken place?
2 Is it reasonable to accept miracles as part of a religious view of life?
3 How should accounts of miracles be understood, if they are to be more than simply violations of a law of nature?

2 Hume on evidence and miracles

KEY ISSUE

● If a miracle is defined as a violation of a law of nature, it is always going to be more likely that you were misled than that it actually happened

---

David Hume (1711–1776) pointed out that scientific laws were not true universal statements, but only summaries of what had been experienced so far. The very method used – gathering data and drawing general conclusions from it – yielded higher and higher degrees of probability, but there was no way of moving from this to absolute certainty. Whether something should be believed or not therefore depended upon the strength of the evidence for or against it being true. It is illustrated by his approach to miracles, which he takes to be violations of a law of nature.

His argument, which clearly illustrates the empirical approach so central to the science of his day, comes in three parts:

1 on evidence

> A wise man… proportions his belief to the evidence. In such conclusions are founded upon an infallible experience, he expects the event with the last degree of assurance, and regards his past experience as a full *proof* of the future existence of the event. In other cases he proceeds with more caution: He weighs the opposite experiments: He considers which side is supported by the greater number of experiments; to that side he inclines, with doubt and hesitation; and when at last he fixes his judgement, the evidence exceeds not what we properly call probability… A hundred instances or experiments on one side, and fifty on another, afford a doubtful expectation of any event; though a hundred uniform experiments, with only one that is contrary, reasonably beget a pretty strong degree of assurance.

2 on believing the testimony of others

> We frequently hesitate concerning the reports of others… We entertain a suspicion concerning any matter of fact, when the witnesses contradict each other; when they are few, or of a doubtful character; when they have an interest in what they affirm; when they deliver their

testimony with hesitation, or on the contrary, with too violent asserverations. There are many other particulars of the same kind which may diminish or destroy the force of any argument derived from human testimony.

3   on miracles

A miracle is a violation of the laws of nature; and as a firm and unalterable experience has established these laws, the proof against a miracle, from the very nature of the fact, is as entire as any argument from experience can possibly be imagined... The plain consequence is (and it is a general maxim worthy of our attention), 'That no testimony is ever sufficient to establish a miracle, unless the testimony be of such a kind that its falsehood would be more miraculous than the fact which it endeavours to establish;'... When anyone tells me, that he saw a dead man restored to life, I immediately consider with myself. whether it be more probable, that this person should either deceive or be deceived, or that the fact, which he relates, should really have happened.

from his *An Enquiry into Human Understanding*

His argument thus involved four steps:

1   to be a miracle an event must violate a law of nature
2   to know if something has taken place, one must weigh evidence for and against
3   laws of nature are based on the maximum available evidence
4   there can never be sufficient evidence to show that a miracle has taken place, since it will always be more likely (on empirical grounds) that a witness was mistaken, than that a law of nature was broken.

This does not imply that a miracle **cannot** take place, simply **that there can never be sufficient evidence to show that it has**.

The Roman Catholic Church regards it as important to establish whether there is evidence to establish that a miracle has taken place. The Vatican's 'Congregation for the Causes of the Saints' examines evidence for miracles, and a person can generally only be declared to be a saint (canonised) if miracles can be shown to have taken place as a result of requesting their help in prayer. Such examination involves the calling of witness and may take several years to complete. Therefore, whatever interpretations may be offered for the term 'miracle', the idea that it represents an event for which there is no natural explanation is still religiously significant.

3 Reasonably miraculous?

Scientific laws are **descriptive**, not **prescriptive**. In other words, the 'laws of nature' cannot in any way dictate what must happen; they merely summarise what has been found to happen in the past. Based on such summaries, of course (assuming that nature is uniform in the way it operates), it is possible to predict what will happen in exactly similar situations in the future.

Strictly speaking, a 'violation of a law of nature' is impossible. You can violate a prescriptive law, simply by refusing to obey it; but how can you violate what is no more than a summary of your past action? If an event cannot be explained in terms of the existing 'laws', then the assumption is made that either our evidence for that event is incorrect, or that some other law is at work, and that this event is an example of that as-yet-unknown set of circumstances.

We have seen, for example, that quantum physics has shown that many of the principles of Newtonian physics are inadequate to deal with the sub-atomic level. That has not overthrown Newton, nor has the action of sub-atomic particles been deemed miraculous. All that has happened is that Newtonian physics is shown to be valid only within a limited set of conditions.

It is also important to recognise that an event can be unique. In one sense, every event is unique, in that it takes place at a particular time and place and as a result of circumstances which will never be exactly the same again. On the other hand, science works by abstracting the most significant factors in each event, and making its predictions based on them – so that many events will be similar enough to one another to form the basis for a hypothesis. Thus, for example, you may watch an apple fall from a tree as a basis for ideas about gravity, but it is irrelevant whether the apple is green or red.

Certain events are unique in the sense that they are found at extreme conditions that cannot be encountered more than once. The 'big bang' at the origin of the known universe is the most clear example of this. It can survive within a scientific theory about the origin of the universe, even though it cannot be compared with other 'big bangs' in other universes.

There are other situations – such as the 'event horizon' beyond which matter vanished into a 'black hole' due to the effect of extreme gravity – that are radically different from what can be found elsewhere in the universe. That does not stop scientists examining them, nor framing hypotheses relevant to them.

We need to be clear about the following:

- science does not deny that an event can be unique
- science does not automatically rule out the possibility that an event may not be covered by existing 'laws of nature'
- science makes progress at exactly those points where existing theories fail to account for an occurrence. The task of science is to show the inadequacies of existing theories, and to frame better ones that take apparent anomalies into account.

The crucial point is whether the interpretation offered for an event is reasonable given existing knowledge and the evidence available. There is a general (and very wise) philosophical principle (known as

Okham's razor) that, if there are two or more explanations for an event, you should always incline to the simplest or most straightforward. On this principle, the general criticism of any miraculous interpretation, from a scientific point of view, is that it does not represent the most **likely** explanation of an event.

4 Redefining the miraculous

Another important issue for 'miracles' in the science and religion debate is what the direct action of God might mean in a world where events are given a scientific explanation. Can an event be called a miracle if it is also fully explicable in scientific terms? What is the significance of calling something a miracle?

It is possible, for example, to argue that accounts of miracles should not be taken literally: in 1670, **Spinoza** criticised the credulity of those who saw 'miracles' as evidence for the existence of God. He argued that the miracle stories in the Bible were not recorded to satisfy the reason, but to stimulate the religious imagination. They were **symbolic** rather than literal.

In the 19th century, some theologians offered natural explanations for Biblical miracles (e.g. Bahrdt's idea that Jesus might have been walking towards the boat on a huge submerged timber in John 6:12, rather than literally walking on water). Others (e.g. D F Strauss, *The Life of Jesus*, 1835) argued that miracle stories were **mythical**: literary devices for expressing the significance of Jesus.

The philosopher Feuerbach (1804–1872) saw accounts of miracles as projections of human desires – they described what people longed for, or thought should happen, rather than what did actually happen. In this sense they could be important emotionally and even religiously, but not factually.

Non-literal interpretations of miracles given by modern theologians tend to emphasise the significance of miracles in terms of the values and qualities they depict, and the coded references found in them (e.g. walking on the water and calming a storm might be taken in the context of ascribing divinity to Jesus – such things being a sign of acting with the power of the Creator) rather than in terms of their being events with no known cause. **Thus, even if it could be proved by overwhelming evidence that a man walked on the water two thousand years ago, that action in itself, without further interpretation, would have no importance whatsoever. Only once the event is given an interpretation does it become significant.**

For reflection:
In 1988, samples of the material of the Turin Shroud (which was believed to bear the image of Jesus and to have been the cloth in which he was wrapped following the crucifixion) were taken for carbon dating at three separate laboratories in Tuscon, Oxford and

Zurich. All three concluded that the Turin Shroud was a mediaeval forgery, dating from between 1260 and 1390. Yet by the time it next went on display in April 1998, hundreds of thousands of people had already made telephone bookings, coming to Turin Cathedral from all over the world to see this 'miraculous' image of Jesus. What does that say about the concept of 'miracle'?

5 Miracles and the arguments for the existence of God

KEY ISSUE

● Does the idea of miracles undermine the traditional proofs for the existence of God?

Two important arguments for the existence of God depend upon a sense of the regularity and purposefulness in nature. The **cosmological** argument sees God as the uncaused cause or unmoved mover, providing an explanation for **all** movement or change. The **teleological** argument sees God as a designer, explaining why it is that things in this world work together in a way that appeared difficult to account for in terms of blind chance. If nature were not predictable or purposeful, if events appeared haphazard or unrelated to one another, then the idea of a creator god would become problematic. How then does the idea of the miraculous relate to this predictable, purposeful universe?

For a theist, it is important that **everything** that happens is the will of God, and that nothing is outside his knowledge or control. That is the implication of the two central attributes of God – omniscience and omnipotence. But if that is the case, miracles would seem to be redundant; worse, they would be a sign of God becoming inconsistent in his behaviour, changing his mind at whim. If one person survives a crash that kills a hundred, why should that survival be deemed a 'miracle' performed by God, when (if God is omnipotent) the deaths of the hundred are equally willed by him?

This problem applies whether or not the concept of miracle is taken literally as 'a violation of a law of nature'. If it is literal, then God appears inconstant and the teleological and cosmological arguments lose their force. But if it is non-literal (in other words, if the term 'miracle' is used as an interpretation of an event which might otherwise be given a natural explanation), one needs to ask why a believer would ascribe significance to that one event rather than all others – for God would be responsible for all equally.

Richard Dawkins (in *Climbing Mount Improbable* and elsewhere) has argued that nature is indeed awesome and creative – the intricacies of life are to be wondered at, and the way they have developed is quite amazing. But he sees no justification in going beyond that fact to posit the existence of a creator God. Faced with that challenge, some believers might be tempted to call on special providence (see pages 102–4) or miracles as a proof of God's existence, by claiming that he shows himself in particular actions. By doing so they have cut away the very basis of the theistic arguments, for by making God particular and his action localised, they have all but admitted that Dawkins is correct in finding the **general** creativity in the world is not in itself sufficient to prove a divine creator.

> **NOTE**   The problem of evil is another direct consequence of the concept of 'miracle'. If God has determined that the world shall be such that it shall contain the possibilities of suffering and death on an appalling scale, then can he be 'good', or indeed, can he exist at all? The argument that in particular cases (miracles) the expected suffering is set aside, points to a capricious God, and not one who can be thought of as a creator of the universe.

Summary List

- If a miracle is defined as a violation of a law of nature, evidence is overwhelmingly against it
- Miracles are events that have particular significance, irrespective of their inherent unlikeliness
- It is illogical to use the regularity of nature as proof of the existence of God, and then use an apparent violation of that regularity for the same purpose

Essay Questions

1. Can there ever by sufficient evidence to prove that a miracle has taken place? Give your own views on the validity of Hume's argument and on his definition of what constitutes a miracle.
2. Is the idea of a miracle incompatible with that of a God who knows and controls everything? Give your own views and your definition of what constitutes a miracle.
3. Is an interpretation of a miracle that does not involve the violation of a law of nature adequate for religious purposes?

10 Science, God and Evolution

KEYWORDS

providence – the special or general activity of God, providing for the needs of humankind

complexity/consciousness – Teilhard de Chardin's key concept, that a rise in complexity produces a rise in consciousness

1 Purpose and direction

In looking at the history of the development of science and also the methods used by science and religion, it is clear that science is based on a study of evidence for what exists, and the framing of hypotheses concerning the fundamental structures and principles upon which the universe, as we experience it, is formed. It cannot get **beyond** the sphere of the evidence upon which it is based. By contrast, we have seen that religion often makes claims that are not based on empirical evidence. In speaking about God, or an afterlife, it goes beyond the realm of science. Of course, this leaves open the question of whether anything can be known outside experience – in other words, whether there is any valid 'supernatural' knowledge, and how such knowledge might be validated.

As long as science keeps to the analysis of empirical evidence, and religion keeps to personal stories and inspirational concepts which are seen as totally 'beyond' the realm of science, then there are few clashes between them. The real problems occur, however, when religion makes claims that appear to depend upon evidence that can also be examined by science.

We have already seen this in the case of the religious claim that an event is a miracle. It occurs also in the idea of a direction or goal of evolution. **If religion claims that the world is purposeful, it needs to specify that purpose and the evidence for saying that the world is moving to fulfil it. In an evolutionary perspective, the logical place to look for this is at the projected end point of an evolutionary development. In other words, to ask where the world is going.**

2 Background

Much of the background to the issue of finding purpose and direction in the world has already been outlined, since it arose in the context of the development of physics through the 17th and 18th centuries, and evolution in the 19th century.

Some scientists and philosophers took the view that religion would be replaced by science – and that the practical consequences of scientific discovery would offer humankind a better future and a worthy goal. In the 19th century, Herbert Spencer, who considered the implications for humanity of the idea of evolution, largely dismissed religion as simply concerned with the unknowable, and Haeckel mocked the idea of a God as 'a gaseous vertebrate' (in other words, an impossibility). Other thinkers, taking religion more seriously, still saw it as a limited phase in humankind's self-understanding. Frazer (author of *The Golden Bough*, a huge exploration of religion and culture) saw three stages in human development:

1 Magic – through which people try to manipulate nature
2 Religion – belief in supernatural powers that rule the world
3 Science – leading to human self-reliance, based on observation.

As humanity develops, therefore, religion is likely to diminish.

The scientist Ernst Mach (1838–1916) argued that all knowledge must stem from sense data, and wanted to see a unification of the physical, biological and psychological sciences, and Pearson (in *The Grammar of Science*, 1892) insisted that the scientific method was the only way to knowledge. Haeckel too was able to celebrate the massive advances of science by the turn of the century. Then, early in the 20th century, came 'logical positivism' and the argument that only statements that could be verified by empirical evidence were meaningful – a view based very much on the obvious success in the physical sciences.

These things, taken together, represented a general growth in the view that science could offer (in theory, if not in practice) an overall explanation of the world, without reference to the idea of God. Meanwhile 'God' was relegated to the subjective feelings of believers, or the projected aspirations of society – as we saw in the chapter on the interpretation of religion from the standpoint of psychology and sociology.

How then have religious thinkers responded?

3 God, evolution and creationism

KEY ISSUE
- The way in which belief in God relates to the process of, or direction of, evolution

Already, in connection with 19th century developments, we have looked at some of the implications of Darwin's work. The key factor being the mechanism (natural selection), by which change in the direction of apparent 'design' could come about without the need for an external designer. **Creationists**, holding to a literal (or near literal) interpretation of scripture, may accept that one thing was created before another, but will usually argue that this is implied by the 6 'days' of creation in Genesis – each day being taken to refer to a long period of time, rather than a literal 24 hour period. What Creationists want to preserve is the uniqueness of the creation of humankind, and the direct action of God to bring it about.

From a scientific point of view, creationism is simply wrong, for it makes a distinction between human and other species which is simply not in line with the common body of genetic information through which all species are formed. Species are not as different from one another as creationists wish to assert.

If the creationists are wrong, and the world has been formed through a process of evolution, how may religious people relate this to the idea of God? (See, for example, J Greer, *Evolution and God*, for a full discussion of this.) There are a number of possibilities here:

- A theistic 'interventionist' approach suggests that, although evolution can account for the development of species, there are moments when God intervenes directly. Thus, for example, the official Catholic teaching (in Humani Generis, 1950) stated that the body of Adam may have been developed by a process of natural selection from other species, but that his soul was created directly by God. (We shall see in the next chapter the problems associated with this view.) One of the problems here is that it sees God as occupying a 'gap' in scientific explanation, and – as we have seen – this creates further problems as science gradually extends human knowledge.

- A different approach, but also one taken from a Catholic standpoint, comes from Karl Rahner (in *Hominisation*, 1965), who argues that human beings are made wholly by evolution, but also – from a religious point of view – wholly by God. In such an approach, God and evolution are not seen as mutually exclusive explanations of human origins, but evolution is seen as a mechanism through which God operates.

- The philosopher Henri Bergson (1859-1941) argued, in his book *Creative Evolution*, that there was a 'life force' guiding the evolutionary process, and that this propelled all species forward in a great movement towards the future. This view is generally termed **vitalism**, and at one time it was thought to provide a way of seeing the action of God within the evolutionary process. However, developments in 20th century biology, showing the basis for evolution to be by random genetic mutation, make the idea of a 'life force' redundant.

- It is also possible to see evolution itself as having a definite purpose and direction through the interpretation given of it by religion. In this way science and religion complement one another in their assessment of the evolutionary process. Examples of this are found in A Peacocke, *Science and the Christian Experiment*, and Birch, *Nature and God* – who see God's activity as determining the 'final causes' of everything (to use terminology originally coined by Aristotle. An interesting version of this approach is that taken by Teilhard de Chardin, which is set out in the next section.

All of these approaches raise a fundamental dilemma, which appears time and again in religion and science debates. How it is possible to relate an autonomous universe with what religious people want to claim as the action of God?

4 The future of humankind

KEY ISSUE

● Is it possible to specify the future direction of evolution in a way that includes a religious ideal?

Teilhard de Chardin (1881–1955), a Jesuit priest and a scientist (a palaeontologist), was concerned to reconcile the very positive view of humankind's future that he found within the scientific community with Christian faith. In particular, he believed that Christianity should promote the future of life on Earth, rather than being concerned primarily with some 'spiritual' goal beyond it. His basic question was: 'How can Christ be related to the ultimate goal of the evolution of humankind, such that I can serve him by helping to build the world of tomorrow?'

By observation of the way in which early life forms developed, Teilhard came to formulate what he called 'the law of complexity/consciousness.' He considered that, at the very basis of the evolutionary process were simple atoms, but these joined with others to become molecules, then joined again to become more complex mega-molecules, like the proteins. Beyond that, even more complex arrangements started to form as cells, and from then on you have increasing complexity as you go up the evolutionary tree of life, finally reaching humankind. Humans have more intelligence and self-awareness than other creatures, because they are the most complex beings yet produced by this process of ever-more-complex, convergent evolution.

The overall principle he saw in this was that **the more complex an organism became, the more consciousness it possessed**. He therefore argued that the process of evolution could be seen as a cone. At the base are individual atoms, then, as these come closer together you work your way up through molecules and cells, to the emergence of humankind. Then he sees the process continuing up the cone. Just as atoms become part of molecules, so individuals become part of something greater, with Christ appearing as mankind comes together. Whereas the spreading of life over the limited surface of the planet creates a 'biosphere', so he sees communication and thought spreading over the surface of the earth and becoming ever more complex, in what he terms the 'noosphere' (from the Greek word for mind). The noosphere cannot expand indefinitely, since the surface of the globe is finite, so humankind comes together (e.g. through increasing communication and travel) until it reaches a point of complete unity, which faith then describes as the universal Christ. Notice, of course, that this is not Jesus of Nazareth, but the Christ spoken of by St Paul, in *Ephesians* – the Christ who is to take everything up into himself. **He calls this goal of evolution 'Omega'.**

Notice that this attempts to 'locate' the object of religious devotion in a way that fits in with an evolutionary perspective. Just as Aquinas presented God as the 'unmoved mover' lying behind and making possible all that came into existence, so Teilhard effectively places God (in the person of Christ) at the end point of a process of convergent evolution, with Christ as the central axis.

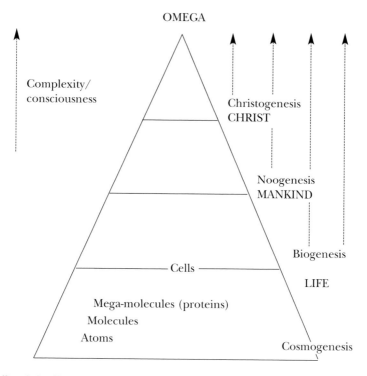

Teihard de Chardin's cone diagram of complexity/consciousness

A major problem with this sort of theory is that it is a mixture of science and religious vision, and it allows the two sorts of language and proof to flow into one another. Thus his best-known book *The Phenomenon of Man* has a great deal of scientific 'evidence' about the progress of evolution, but it also contains religious views about the Universal Christ which cannot be considered as the conclusions of a scientific argument.

Teilhard may therefore be criticised from both a religious point of view (since he appears to make the appearance of the Universal Christ dependent upon a particular view of evolution) and also from a scientific point of view (for trying to reach religious conclusions from scientific evidence, and going beyond what can be proved).

What Teilhard was trying to do was to fuse a scientific view of evolution and the future with the religious need for a personal and spiritual goal. Many might agree that it would be ideal if one's scientific view of the future coincided with one's religious goal, but that is not the same thing as trying to use the one to prove the other.

5 Providence

> **KEY ISSUE**
>
> ● Is belief in divine providence reasonable in the light of evolution and the sufferings of contingent existence?

A key religious term for the discussion of purpose and direction is 'providence.' This is the belief that God has in some way chosen to create, nurture and sustain humankind: that life is not possible merely by some chance, or by the impersonal process of evolution, but is something guided by God for his own purpose in dealing with humankind. Some religious thinkers make this a key factor in their understanding of God. In his book *Science and Providence* (1989), John Polkinghorne comments:

> Though the evolutionary history of life has proved marvellously fertile, it shows scant concern for individual species, let alone particular creatures... Without the special providence, the idea of a personal God is emptied of content. Whatever it may mean to use personal language of God in an analogical sense, it surely cannot mean less than we experience of our own personhood, which is not content with general benevolence but seeks to meet individual needs in individual ways.

In other words, it is not enough to accept a general providence – that God in some way established the evolutionary process in order to create humankind – but a personal creator would want to react to particular situations.

The religious difficulty with the idea of special providence is that it attempts to ascribe divine purpose to some events but not to others. Thus, if an aircraft crashes, killing all but one of its occupants, the lone survivor might ascribe his or her survival to divine providence. But that same act of special providence (given the idea of an omnipotent God) implies responsibility for the death of all the others. **Those who feel themselves specially selected, can do so only at the expense of others who are not so favoured.**

Every claim for special providence implies a selective field of vision or interest. Thus, from the point of view of mammals in general and human beings in particular, the destruction of the dinosaurs might seem to have been providential. But if that is the case, then surely another species, now awaiting its chance to flourish, may herald the destruction of the human species in exactly the same way. **Winning a lottery is providential only in the eyes of the person who actually wins!**

The implication of this for the whole issue of God and evolution is therefore clear. Evolution provides the structure, the machinery, by which species develop. It is a process by which random changes afford an opportunity for some individuals in a species to develop more than others, to reproduce more successfully, and thus to influence future generations and the gradual shift in the character of the species.

In the eyes of a secular scientist like Richard Dawkins, that process is magnificent and utterly awe-inspiring. The most complex and wonderful creatures emerge from a long process which involves the application of just a few basic principles. That spectacle of self-generated life does not require an external creator. Equally, it makes little sense, given the huge 'wastage' of life that is involved in every evolutionary advance, to ascribe its direction to the special intervention of God. However, Polkinghorne concludes:

> The Christian understanding of providence steers a course between a facile optimism and a fatalistic pessimism. God does not fussily intervene to deliver us from all discomfort but neither is he the impotent beholder of cosmic history. Patiently, subtly, with infinite respect for the creation with which he has to deal, he is at work within the flexibility of its process.

Science and Providence, p44

Of course, the key question here is exactly how you tell the difference between a patient and subtle providence and no providence at all! At what point (Auschwitz; the 1999 earthquake in Turkey; a single child dying of cancer) would it have been 'fussy' for God to have intervened?

6 Some reflections

We have looked at a number of ways in which God and evolutionary science can be related:

- **either** the world is materially determined and wonderfully self-creating, and there is no God (except in the religious imagination, as a way of interpreting the world);
- **or** science is wrong when its conclusions differ from the teaching of the Bible, and evolution is either a mistaken theory, or has limited scope;
- **or** evolution explains the mechanism by which the world has developed, and God can be understood as being involved within, or as underlying that process.

In evaluating these options, you may wish to consider the following questions:

1 What does religion mean by the 'supernatural'? Does the supernatural have to be totally **outside** the realm of natural causes? Is the supernatural necessary for religion?
2 God is spoken of as being both transcendent and immanent. How might the idea of immanence be used to show God **within** the evolutionary process?
3 In a sacrament, God is described as being present and active in an event which has a physical basis. Is it possible therefore to describe the relationship between God and the whole evolving world as 'sacramental'?

S L Jaki, in *Cosmos and Creator*, 1980, argued that there is no way in which we can decide, from evidence alone, between blind mechanism and purposeful mechanism; purpose can only be seen once there is a prior belief in God as the rational creator. The world, as revealed by science, is contingent (i.e. it need not have existed at all), and in itself it appears to be meaningless. The world can only be thought of as a 'home', a rationally ordered cosmos, if a person first accepts the idea that it has a creator. This is linked to the main theme of Jaki's work, which is that science makes no sense without the belief that the world is a rationally ordered place, capable of being understood. He sees this as the common basis of natural theology and science.

One of the criticisms brought against Teilhard de Chardin was that he appeared to force the idea of evolutionary direction to fit his religious goal of Omega, rather than accepting the possibility that evolution might prove to be directionless.

Here there is a particular example of the old question about the extent to which our ideas shape the world we experience. Until the 19th century, it was generally accepted that the scientific method was as 'objective' as possible, and that evidence should not be distorted by the particular views of the scientist. That view has been modified during the last century only to the extent that it is recognised that the way in which we observe data influences that which we observe. That caveat applies generally to the extremes of our experience – notably the area of sub-atomic particles. It cannot be taken as a general retreat from the attempt to assess evidence in an impartial way.

It is important to take into account, however, the function of religion in giving a sense of meaning and purpose. Its statements are **interpretations** of the world as much as claims about particular things **in** the world – and **interpreting the significance and value of something is a personal activity that need not conflict with the sort of evidence relevant to science**.

The three questions given above raise fundamental issues about the nature of religious claims. Key to these is the question about what is meant by 'supernatural'. If it denotes causes and explanations which are conceived of as being of the same kind as those found within the universe, but somehow external to it, then the general view of science will always be that there can be no evidence for such things, and that the scientific view of the world sees no need to take them into account. On the other hand, if 'supernatural' is taken in some way to mean an interpretation of, or way of encountering, the world, then there seems to be no reason why it should not exist alongside scientific explanations, since the two modes of thought and explanation are quite different.

For example:
Falling in love with someone can be exhaustively described in terms of psychological and biological urges, the operation of hormones and genetic predispositions and perhaps even social pressures. Yet such a description cannot do justice to the actual experience. It is not that there is 'something else' that is love. Love is simply the personal way of describing what happens. This distinction is common enough (described in terms of analysis or synthesis, of taking a reductionist or holistic view) but it remains central to these issues. To present God's creativity as somehow an **alternative** to evolution is doing the equivalent of making love an alternative to hormones.

Finally, we should note the implications of the evolutionary theory for aspects of human life. Darwin's theory of natural selection commented that it was, in fact, the most well-adapted of each species which tended to survive and reproduce. He did not say that the fittest **should** survive, merely that they **did** survive. It was clearly possible – as in the thinking of Spencer, who coined the term 'survival of the fittest' – to see that the theory of evolution could be applied to human society.

It is therefore understandable (but illogical) to use natural selection as a theory to justify the strong not being held back by the weak. In other words, that the natural mechanism of evolution should be made prescriptive. We see this, although not specifically linked to Darwin, in the ideas of Nietzsche, whose morality was shaped by the human desire to progress towards a form of higher self.

An entirely different approach, but equally significant for morality, is that taken by Richard Dawkins in his early book *The Selfish Gene*, 1976, in which he argues that human beings are survival suits created for the continuation of human genes.

This does not imply that everyone should act in a competitive way. There are cases where genuine altruism may, in the long run, be better for the survival of a group or species than the 'survival of the fittest'. Thus, giving one's life to save another member of the same group may be deeply engrained into the human psyche simply in order to benefit the group's genetic chances. On this basis, morality is a natural method of getting us to function better together, and thus improve our long-term survival strategy.

Summary List

- Religion seeks meaning and purpose, but it is difficult to specify a 'purpose' for evolution without being able to define its end point
- Teilhard de Chardin, in arguing for a goal of evolution that fitted his religious aspirations (Christ Omega), produced a scheme that he found religiously satisfying, but which could not be justified scientifically
- The idea of divine providence raises questions about suffering and the nature of evolution
- Natural selection is descriptive, not prescriptive, and cannot therefore be used as a valid basis for a moral stance

Essay Questions

1. Is evolution compatible with the idea of divine providence?
2. To what extent is it valid to link a religious idea to a scientific theory? Illustrate your answer with reference to Teilhard de Chardin's view of evolution leading towards Christ at Omega.
3. Do you consider the structure of the universe, or the final outcome of its evolution to be relevant to the Christian faith?

11 Humankind

KEYWORDS

reductionist – the view that complex entities are nothing more than the sum total of their constituent parts

holistic – an approach that considers complex entities as whole individual units

genome – the chemical sequence of genetic information strung out along DNA

immortality – the belief that part of a human being does not die

resurrection – the belief that, after death, God raises human beings to life

reincarnation – the belief that a self or soul can pass on to another body after death

re-becoming – the Buddhist view that human beings, like all complex entities, are constantly changing

1 Examining humankind

KEY ISSUES
- **Reductionist approaches** analyse human beings into their constituent cells and atoms
- **Holistic approaches** deal with the human being as a whole, considering issues of personality and relationships which cannot be seen in terms of analysis into simpler levels of reality

There are two very different approaches to understanding what a human being is. In a **reductionist** analysis, complex entities are reduced to their component parts. Therefore, I am nothing more than the sum total of all the cells of which my body is made. Each of those cells is nothing more than the atoms of which it is composed. Each atom is nothing more than the sum of the particles, or quarks, of which it is comprised.

The analysis of objects in this way also implies that one branch of science can be reduced to another. Biology is concerned with living cells, but these can be reduced to the compounds of which they are made (chemistry) and finally to the atoms, which follow the laws of physics. In this way, although recognising that they have specialised interests in dealing with very complex entities, biology and chemistry are finally 'reduced' to physics.

The reductionist approach has a direct impact on issues we have already considered, such as freedom and determinism. I may experience freedom, but if the movement of every atom in my body is determined by physical laws, how is that freedom other than an illusion?

In an **holistic** approach, the task is not to reduce a complex entity to its constituent parts, but to see what the distinctive features of that entity are – features that can only appear because of its complexity. Holistic approaches recognise that different principles operate at different levels of complexity and identity.

What then is a human being? We can consider this question from these two different approaches: reductionist and holistic.

- From a **reductionist** point of view, as is often pointed out, a human being can be seen as forty five litres of water, plus carbon, iron, phosphorous, fats, all organised harmoniously by the genetic code in the DNA. The human being is a marvel of complexity and organisation. Like jumbled pieces of a jigsaw puzzle in their box, you know that somehow all these molecules and atoms must fit together to form the single human image, but how they manage to do so is quite astounding.
- From the **holistic** point of view, a human being relates to others, thinks, chooses, wills, dreams, plans the future and suffers from events in the past. This complex entity exhibits a form of life that is of a different order from that of its constituent molecules.

Of course, the two ways of looking are not mutually exclusive. What happens at the level of individual cells can influence the whole person (e.g. when cells reproduce out of control, and a life-threatening cancer develops). Equally, a holistic event (e.g. getting excited about something) has an immediate effect on many of the body's systems.

Clearly, religion functions at the holistic level. It is not concerned primarily with the way in which DNA controls particular cells, but with the behaviour and beliefs of individual people. A key question is whether human behaviour and beliefs at the holistic level is controlled by operations at the genetic level, rendering language about personal choice or morality meaningless. This was highlighted, for example, by issues raised in Richard Dawkin's early book *The Selfish Gene*, considering the prospect that humans behave in ways that reflect the needs of their genes to thrive and continue to reproduce.

a) The place of human life

In the medieval world view, the Earth was central to the universe, and everything had a purpose related to human destiny. This followed the biblical view that God had created Man and given him authority over all other creatures.

Following the rise of modern science, it became increasingly clear that the universe was far larger than had been thought, and everything was seen as controlled by impersonal laws that had no relationship to human needs. Consequently the centrality of humankind was threatened.

Cosmologies of the 20th century have only heightened the awesomeness of the universe. Humankind may claim to have a significant role to play within the scheme of evolution on this planet, but when our solar system is lost among millions of others, the universe seems totally devoid of anything that could appear as providence or purpose related to humanity.

One of the functions of religious stories of creation was to 'place' humankind within the universe, giving to our species a sense of purpose. It is that basic function that is threatened by an impersonal universe in which humanity is located on a tiny, insignificant planet.

There have been many responses to this, from a traditional religious one in Jaki, *Cosmos and Creator*, through Hoyle's controversial book *The Intelligent Universe*, where he argues for a universal intelligence, to Teilhard de Chardin's attempt to see humankind and Christ as the central axis of evolution.

If, as it is increasingly being celebrated (e.g. by Richard Dawkins in *Unweaving the Rainbow*), science is revealing to us a universe that is awesome both in its size and its complexity, the natural response is to see humankind as correspondingly insignificant. This, of course, is a valid religious response. In the *Book of Job*, God silences Job's complaints by showing him the wonders of the natural world. Faced with such awesome sights, Job's demand that he be immune from suffering, or at least receive an explanation for it, utterly fails.

b) The human machine

In ancient Greece, the natural philosopher **Galen** thought that the purpose of the heart was to create heat, and that air from the lungs stopped the body overheating. Blood was drawn into the right side of the heart, seeped through to the left, was purified, mixed with vital spirits, and then moved off into the arteries. Such was the influence of Galen that Vesalis (in *De Fabrica*, 1538) falsified his own findings in order to make his view of the workings of the body correspond to that of Galen. Nevertheless, it was when this view was challenged by Harvey (*De Motu Cordis*, 1628), who – following nine years of experiments – established that the heart was a pump, and that blood was oxygenated in the lungs before being pumped through the body, that real progress was made in analysing the workings of the human body. It was realised that each organ was nourished by oxygenated blood and the whole body seen as an interconnected system. Individual organs lived because the body as a whole incorporated a system for delivering to them what they needed.

Compare this view with the traditional one of Western religions. In *Genesis*, man is made out of dust (*adamah*) and becomes a living soul (*nephesh*) through receiving the breath of God. A person is therefore fundamentally an animated body, and once God's breath is removed, that person returns to the dust from which he or she was made.

Greek thought went a stage further. Plato thought that a human being comprised an eternal soul (which existed before birth, and would survive death) linked to a physical body. The distinction was made between the physical flesh (*sarx*) which made up the human body (*soma*), which possessed natural life (*psyche*), a thinking element (*nous*) and a spirit (*pneuma*).

Christianity combined the sense of humankind being alive with God's breath, with the distinctions made in Greek thought. The mind and the soul, although linked with the body here on earth, were the bearers of its spiritual destiny. Those who live according to the spirit are contrasted with those whose life is based on the flesh.

The important thing to recognise from all this is that, from a religious point of view, if human beings are to have those things that seem basic to religion – freedom, morality, the spiritual life, the ability to respond to God – they must be considered as 'more than' simply the physical, mechanical body (*sarx*), however complex and awesome its organisation (*soma*) may be.

What is clear is that the elements of human experience that religion features are those that take a **holistic** view – they are to do with **the whole person** and his or her response to life. This need not deny any of the results of analysing the body into its constituent parts, nor does it deny the role of the genes in creating, directing and reproducing the human machine. Rather, it claims that such analysis and genetic functioning is not **the whole** of what human life is about.

2 Human origins

KEY ISSUE

- Evolution shows humankind to be closely related to other species, and to be a very recent arrival in terms of the evolution of life on Earth

---

In the 19th century, as we saw, the theory of evolution was a key feature of the debate between religion and science, with Darwin's natural selection seen as a threat not only to the creativity of God but also to the place of humankind within the natural order. With the appreciation of genetics, the balance has shifted somewhat by the overall recognition that the genetic make-up of humans is not significantly different from the other species to which they are closely related, and that – whatever their origins – they are well integrated into the web of life that embraces all species. Thinking of humankind as a separate 'afterthought', added to an existing world of plants and animals, is simply to go against the fundamental insights of modern biology.

Another feature of genetics, applied to human origins, shows that the idea of humankind starting with a single original couple, Adam and Eve (an idea termed **monogenism**, or the **Adamic theory**), is very improbable. For this to have taken place would require a mutant couple (i.e. a pair sharing exactly the same mutations) who were also sufficiently different from the rest of their species to prevent interbreeding. Whereas the more normal way for a new species to become established is for the gradual accumulation of differences in one group to separate them off from the rest of their species, as sometimes happens through geographical separation.

Nevertheless, it is still valuable to reflect on the relative age of the human species compared with that of the Earth, which at about 5 billion years is around one third of the age of the universe itself.

- Vegetation and dry land: 410 million years ago
- Major destructions of existing species: 250 million years ago (approx 90% species destroyed) and 65 million years ago (the dinosaurs and approx 50% of other species destroyed).
- Mammals: 50 million years ago
- First apes: 35 million years ago
- Australopitheci: 4 million years ago (brain capacity increases from 450 to 750cc)
- Homo erectus: 700,000 years – found in Africa, Asia and Europe (brain capacity 800 to 1200 cc), shaping stones and using fire
- Neanderthal Man: 75,000 years, burial places and funeral rites
- Home Sapiens: 40,000 years (brain capacity reaches 1400cc – as modern man) paintings and language
- First settlements in the Fertile Crescent of the Middle East: 10,000 years.

Whatever questions are raised about human origins, the figures given above (which are very approximate and are open to scientific challenge) at least put the very brief period of time during which human beings have lived on Earth into some sort of perspective.

It is also worth noting (again, to get human life into perspective) that major destructions of species – although not on the scale of those noted above – occur approximately every 26 million years. (It has been speculated that this could be because of the periodical arrival in our part of the solar system of increased numbers of comets, some of which strike Earth.) Quite apart from the inevitable change in the sun and the inevitable destruction of our planet that it involves, the chances of the species surviving that long would, in any case, be very small indeed.

3 Minds, brains and artificial intelligence

KEY ISSUE

● Is it possible to reproduce the brain artificially and, if so, how would such artificial intelligence relate to the idea of a person, self or soul?

The human brain is the most complex entity known. It consists of about 10^{10} long nerve cells, each connecting with about 10,000 similar cells, their interfaces controlled by chemical messengers. But, however complex and however central to the control of everything in life, the brain is simply one part of the human body, and it is not what religion or philosophy terms the 'soul', 'self' or 'mind'. Naturally, brain activity is closely linked to thought – so that, for example, if someone suffers brain damage it affects their ability to think. But that does not mean that we can simply identify the process of thinking with the activity in the brain that takes place as we do it – for that would be to make a reductionist analysis that would hardly do justice to the experience of thought (any more than a huge printout of digits would be a substitute for the music I hear on my CD, even though I know that the CD is actually no more than a way of communicating that sequence of digits).

From all that we have considered so far, it is clear that the sort of human activity with which religion is concerned – thinking, choosing, valuing, celebrating, sympathising, worshipping – is not easily recognised once it has been through a process of reductionist analysis. I may accept, for example, that a chimpanzee shares 99% of its genetic material with a human being, and at that level they are very similar creatures. On the other hand, when it comes to matters of philosophy, religion and ethics, the species appear to be utterly different; the chimpanzee lacks those very distinctive human qualities and abilities which make reflective thought and religion possible. The reason for this difference between humans and their close genetic neighbours may lie in brain capacity: 400cc for the chimp compared with the human 1400cc. However it is probably not simply a matter of brains, for we know that people's behaviour and attitude can change as a result of a whole variety of things – the environment within which they life, the food and drink they consume, the various stimuli they receive. Emotions are as much about chemistry as they are electrical activity in the brain. In other words we need to recognise that the brain is simply one part of a set of physical connections that link us with the rest of the universe. It may integrate and process all the stimuli that we receive, it may control what we think and do, we may even identify which parts of the brain control particular human skills and attitudes; but that does not identify the brain with the 'self' any more than a drive in the countryside can be identified with the workings of the car we use.

The dilemma is how you identify the 'self' if it is neither the brain, nor any other part of the physical body, and this is a problem for religion in its encounter with science. For example, in 1950 the Roman Catholic Church issued an official statement on evolution (*Humani Generis*) in which it stated that evolution could be discussed as an hypothesis about the development of the physical human body, but that the soul is immediately created by God. This implies a dualism of body and soul, as represented by philosophers like Plato or Descartes. This, of course, is important for any religion that wants to claim that people in some way survive death; there needs to be something that can remain untouched by the physical dissolution of the body.

It is possible, of course, that the mind or soul is simply another, very subtle part of nature. At the end of the 19th century, Haeckel, in trying to show that science was able to vanquish superstition and religion, did not try to deny that there was a 'soul' or that morality was possible, but argued that what people called 'soul' was a natural phenomenon. He was against any idea of a separate realm of the spiritual:

> This hypothetical "spirit world," which is supposed to be entirely independent of the material universe, and on the assumption of which the whole artificial structure of the dualistic system is based, is purely a product of the poetic imagination; the same must be said of the parallel belief in the "immortality of the soul," the scientific impossibility of which we must prove more fully later on....
>
> Our own naturalistic conception of the psychic activity sees in it a group of vital phenomena which are dependent on a definite material substratum, like all other phenomena...

> *The Riddle of the Universe*, p74

A great deal has happened in science since Haeckel's day, and a present-day scientist is likely to speak about these things rather differently. But there is one element in his argument that remains relevant: he points out that psychic activity depends on a 'definite material substratum'. Is it possible, therefore, in constructing an appropriate 'material substratum', to produce psychic activity – in other words, can you build something that takes on human qualities and characteristics?

Here we touch on the issue of artificial intelligence. The more complex something is, the more personal and spontaneous it appears. Early computers were very crude; they processed sets of instructions in a methodical way, but not one that appeared in any way to display creativity. But increase memory and processor speed and the interaction of operator and computer starts to become more like the interaction between two individuals.

Artificial Intelligence is a fascinating subject, and very relevant for the issues of religion and science. On the one hand, it becomes increasingly difficult to define exactly what it is that computers cannot do that would be necessary for them to be considered to be thinking and relating in a human way. On the other, it is clear that a computer is only as good as the information programmed into it, and that programming depends on human beings. Thus the computer can be seen as no more than a mechanical tool – albeit a very clever one that can reflect back the intelligence and personality of its human creators. But this should not allow human beings to remain smug, for they too are programmed. The whole world of language and thought, whatever our latent disposition to develop it, is something we are taught. Our language and ideas do not arrive in our heads from nowhere – they are a response to our human environment. Is this so very different from the process whereby a computer is programmed?

4 The human genome

One of the most fascinating developments in work in this field is the analysis of the human genome – the sequence of 3 billion chemical units called 'bases' (groups of which form 'genes') that are strung out along the human DNA. About 70,000 of these genes produce proteins, and thus provide the instructions that are needed to make a human being. In identifying the genes responsible for particular human defects, and also the way in which the body controls the reproduction of cells, it is hoped that medicine will be transformed.

Thus, for example, if a growth-controlling gene in the DNA in a cell becomes damaged, that cell may reproduce in an irregular way. The body's defence mechanism generally spots the damage and produces a protein that inhibits the cell from reproducing until the DNA is repaired. If, for some reason, that protein is not produced, the mutant cell may reproduce out of control, and a cancer is formed. Discovery of the gene responsible for that protein inhibitor might lead to a treatment for cancer in which patients would be given that gene protein so that the body could use a natural means of curing itself, stopping the reproduction of the cancer cells.

Some diseases are inherited, so that a person is born with a particular gene damaged. It is hoped that eventually such damaged genes may be replaced, countering the disease, but gene therapy of this sort is still being developed.

The greatest significance of the Human Genome Project (the task of identifying each of the genes on the human genome) is that it will provide a vast amount of information about how the body works at the genetic level. That information may be of value in ways that we cannot yet imagine.

Recent debates on genetically modified foods illustrate the moral (and therefore religious) issues that come from this new technology. This debate will become even more significant once technologies that stem from work on the human genome are widespread.

The perspective offered by this is that the development of a human individual depends on the transmission of information at the moment of conception. **This is not the same as the reductionist approach – seeing an individual in terms of his or her component cells – for it reveals the 'form' of the individual, the key that enables that complex entity to take shape. To use an analogy: if the music of a symphony may be 'reduced' to vibrations in the air, what we have here, by contrast, is the musical score.** That is something quite different from anything known before. How religious and moral thinkers will relate to the potential offered by such information remains to be seen.

5 After death

KEY ISSUE

● The idea of immortality, the Christian doctrine of resurrection and theories of reincarnation and re-becoming, need to be explored in the light of the scientific view of the complexity of a human being

Human immortality depends upon identifying something that transcends the changes of our material environment – for everything that we see and know in this world is contingent (in other words, there was a time when it did not exist in its present form). **Modern cosmology opens up the most amazing vistas, in which energy is transformed into matter, and matter is changed again and again. Thus, the very elements of which we are made were forged in the nuclear reactions within a dying star. Every atom of your body pre-dates the present solar system; you are using them on a very temporary basis.** What are the implications of this for some traditional beliefs?

Immortality cannot depend on our physical existence, for that is extremely temporary. Nor would it make sense to try to identify personal immortality with the fundamental energy of the universe – for that would be to lose all sense of personal identity. The physical re-constitution of a physical body after death is also rather a curious notion, in the light of the way in which the body is constantly changing anyway – for a human being is more a process than a thing.

The main arguments for immortality have traditionally been based on the nature of thought:

- Plato, contrasting particular objects with the ideal 'forms' of which they are examples, believed that we have some innate knowledge of these 'forms' and that such knowledge must have been acquired before birth
- Descartes, in his systematic attempt to doubt everything, concluded 'I think, therefore I am' on the grounds that he could not doubt his own thought. This led to a radical dualism, with matter on one side and mind on the other.

The dilemma with such beliefs is to identify what it is that could survive. Is a disembodied existence possible? What would it be like? Can you have a personality, or even a thought, if you have no body? What would it mean to survive in a non-physical sense?

Of course, such questions are very different from those that one might ask of the traditional Christian concept of life beyond death, which (contrary to popular opinion) is not about immortality but about **resurrection**. Christian belief is that human beings do not possess their own immortality, but receive it from God, who raises them up from death. This is central to the Christian view of Jesus' death and resurrection. It is not that there was a bit of Jesus (his mind?) that somehow survived crucifixion; rather, Christians believe that Jesus did actually die, but then God raised him up. In the same way, they believe that after death, they will be raised up and given a new body. This at least acknowledges the idea that in order to live you need to have a body. The problem it creates is to know how such a new body might be thought of, especially since it cannot be part of the existing world – for that would simply be the re-assembly of existing atoms. However, it is useful here to make the distinction between the Greek terms (see above page 110). The body (*soma*) need not be thought of in crude physical terms (*sarx*).

Some eastern religions take a very different view. The concept of **reincarnation** allows a 'self' to move from body to body – this allows the idea of a self that is not simply identified with its physical body, whilst at the same time acknowledging that it is difficult to see how a self or soul could be said to live on without some sort of body as a vehicle for its self-expression. But reincarnation of this sort still depends on a radical body/soul, or body/mind, dualism.

The only radical religious alternative to this is given in Buddhist thought where everything is in a radical state of change from moment to moment throughout life (in a process generally termed **re-becoming**). What is more (in a teaching called *anatta*, or 'non-self'), it is argued that our separate identity is a conventional, rather than an absolute, way of looking at things. That ultimately, everything connects with everything else, and we are not separate from the ever-changing world that surrounds us. In other words, Buddhism sees each person as part of an on-going process, what they do now contributes to the future, and what they **are** now is the result of a vast number of actions in the past. What Buddhism warns about is the craving to cling on to this present individual life – which it regards as a selfish and futile attitude, and one that can only lead to disappointment.

Beyond this process of change, however, both Hinduism and Buddhism look to a spiritual goal of release (*moksha*), in which the individual in some way leases, and becomes at one with the universal.

Summary List

- Religious and moral aspects of humankind require an holistic rather than a reductionist approach.
- Humankind is closely related to other species, and is a recent arrival in evolutionary terms, contrasting with its privileged place in traditional religious schemes.
- Artificial intelligence can reproduce the operations of the brain, but does not, in itself, function as a human person.
- The human genome can represent a human being, and all the information required for his or her construction, in the form of a sequence of letters. Human development is a matter of the transmission of information.
- Beliefs about existence beyond this life depend upon the relationship of the self with its physical matrix.

Essay Questions

1. Evolution and genetics have undermined the privileged place that humankind has within the universe. Discuss.
2. It will never be possible to construct an artificial self. Do you agree?
   (In responding to this question, please make clear what, if anything, you consider distinctive or essential about a human person.)
3. Of the various religious views about life beyond death, which (if any), in your view, is the most compatible with the scientific view of the self?

Postscript

We have only to look at the history of science to realise that it has the most amazing capacity to surprise.

By the end of the 18th century, the predictable world of Newtonian physics was well established and technology had vindicated the scientific method. Then, in the 19th century, along came Darwin, and suddenly the world was a far more ancient and complex place than had previously been imagined.

However, by the end of that century Haeckel and others could celebrate the triumphs of science, convinced that all the basic groundwork in physics and biology had been established. Then, with the 20th century, came the dramatic changes brought about by relativity and quantum mechanics, and biology became revolutionised by the discovery of DNA and its genetic codes.

In the last decades of that century, information technology developed to the point at which the computing power and technology that had enabled men to walk on the moon in the 1960s, became almost laughably limited, and instant global communication via the internet became routine.

So where are the next scientific advances to be made? The fact is, we can hardly guess at the sort of understanding of themselves and their world that people will have a century from now.

And what of religion? At the end of the 17th century, Toland saw it being stripped of its metaphysical beliefs and made rational and compatible with science. At the end of the 19th, Haeckel mocked it as superstitious and looked to a future dominated by rationality and science. Marx predicted that with the emancipation of the proletariat it would come to an end, and the implication of much of Freud's work is that healthy individuals do not need it.

Yet, at the beginning of the 21st century, it persists. A large percentage of the world's population claim to belong to one of the great religions, at least nominally. And those who do not accept formal religion may nevertheless claim some sort of spirituality and moral sense, exploring those issues about the meaning and purpose of human life with which the religious traditions have been concerned.

Human beings have a great capacity to think, examine and analyse; they also act intuitively, creatively and with a grasp of their place within the whole scheme of things. Neither religion nor science can benefit from a polarisation in which all the thinking is ascribed to science and all the intuition and feeling to religion. Science needs intuition, imagination and feeling as much as religion needs careful thought and a radical honesty in examining the world. Each has much to offer the other.

Further Reading

Recent books, giving substantial coverage of both the historical and contemporary themes, include:
Barbour, Ian G. *Religion and Science* SCM Press, 1998
(This is an updated and expanded version of his earlier *Religion in an Age of Science*, offering a clear exposition of the issues.)
McGrath, Alister E. *Science and Religion: an introduction* Blackwell, 1999
(This is particularly impressive in its very clear and precise coverage of the variety of theological points of view.)
also the 1995/6 Gifford Lectures, published as:
Brooke J & Cantor G. *Reconstructing Nature: The Engagement of Science and Religion* T & T Clarke, 1998

For a substantial standard text on the Philosophy of Science:
Curd, M & Cover J A. *Philosophy of Science: the central issues* Norton & Company, 1998
(This is aimed at undergraduates and is quite demanding but valuable for reference and for examining issues of scientific method.)

For the inspirational perspective on the nature of science and what it reveals, see:
Dawkins, Richard *Unweaving the Rainbow* Penguin, 1998
Dawkins, Richard *Climbing Mount Improbable* Viking, 1996

(Dawkins is not recommended for the religiously faint hearted, since he presents his arguments in a robust way, and does not suffer theological fools gladly.)

or on cosmology, see:
Ferris, Timothy *The Whole Shebang: A state-of-the-universe(s) Report* Weidenfeld & Nicholson, 1997
Hawking, Stephen W. *A Brief History of Time* Bantam Press, 1988

Other useful books on specific issues concerned with religion, include:
Polkinghorne, John *Science and Providence* SPCK, 1989
Polkinghorne, John *Reason and Reality* SPCK, 1991
(These present a clearly argued, traditional Christian position.)

Cupitt, Don *After God* Weidenfeld & Nicholson, 1997
(As a contrast to Polkinghorne, this radical approach explores a naturalistic view of religious belief.)

For a serious re-examination of the view that the universe is uniquely organised with human life as its goal and purpose, a modern 'natural theology', see:
Michael J Denton *Nature's Destiny* The Free Press, 1998

Index